FOUND

FAITHFULLY FLOURISHING

Business Growth Series for Women Entrepreneurs

FAITHFULLY FLOURISHING (Book 1 – Foundation)

Business Growth Series for Women Entrepreneurs

For permissions requests, speaking inquiries, podcast interviews, and bulk order purchase options, email faithfullyflourishingseries@gmail.com.

GingerSteg.com

ISBN: 979-8-9947005-0-1

Cover and Interior Design: Esther Moody

Editing: Lori Lynn Enterprises

CONTENTS

DEDICATION

This journey was prayerfully created with the Bible Babes in mind. May it equip, encourage, and empower you to walk boldly in your God-given calling, both in business and in life. I'm so grateful we get to flourish in faith and purpose together.

An Invitation to
Faithfully Flourish

Many women are carrying responsibility without rest and vision without structure. They are faithful, capable, and generous, yet often weary. *Faithfully Flourishing* exists to remind you that God is a God of order and that stewardship brings peace.

This faith-based book series is designed to help women integrate their faith, calling, and daily work. It brings together Scripture, reflection, prayer, and practical structure so that what you build is rooted in God rather than driven by pressure.

This series will help you flourish spiritually, personally, and practically while remaining grounded in truth and obedience.

"He who began a good work in you will carry it on to completion" (Philippians 1:6).

If you are holding this book, know that it is not by accident. God has drawn you here with intention. This is not simply a workbook or a business resource. It is an invitation to partner with Him in the work He has already begun in you.

Who Is This Book For?

This book is for women who love God and sense that He is calling them to steward something meaningful. You may already be running a business, leading in your home or community, or discerning what God is asking you to build next. You may feel stretched, uncertain, or quietly longing for more alignment and peace.

This book is for the woman who wants her work to matter, not just produce. It is for the woman who desires fruit that lasts.

Faithfully Flourishing is about becoming before doing. It is about stewarding what God has entrusted to you with faith, obedience, and wisdom. It is about building a life and work that reflect His character, His order, and His purpose. This journey is not about hustle or comparison. It is about alignment with Heaven and faithfulness in your current season.

THE STORY BEHIND FAITHFULLY FLOURISHING

I did not set out to build a business or write a series of books. My journey began with a simple desire to live with more purpose and to bring peace and order into spaces that felt overwhelming.

In 2024, while working full-time in the mortgage business, I was also coaching and supporting women inside the GoForth Wellness app alongside my close friend Jenny. A recurring theme kept surfacing: "I don't have time." No time to work out, meal prep, rest, or be consistent. What became clear was that this wasn't a motivation issue or even a wellness issue. It was a time, margin, and stewardship issue.

That's where Time Wise Mastery was born. Through Zoom sessions, one-on-one coaching, and creating courses and workbooks, I began helping women steward their time, energy, and daily rhythms in ways that supported their health, faith, and real-life responsibilities. It wasn't born out of theory, but out of real conversations with real women who loved God and wanted to grow, yet they felt stretched, overwhelmed, and disconnected from peace.

In the midst of this journey, I was part of a local small group called Bible Babes. Week after week, we gathered to open Scripture, share our hearts, pray over one another, and talk honestly about life, faith, and business. In those sacred, ordinary moments of community, something unexpected happened. As we prayed and sought God together, I heard Him clearly impress on my heart the words "Faithfully Flourishing." It was more than a name. It was a divine nudge. A calling. A reminder that flourishing does not come from doing more, but from faithfully walking in obedience with what God has placed in our hands.

Over time, God revealed that what I once thought were separate skills and experiences were actually gifts He had been preparing for His purpose. Planning, time stewardship, leadership, encouragement, and structure were not just productivity tools. They were assignments.

For years, I questioned whether I was qualified. I asked myself who I was to lead or speak into the lives of others. God patiently reminded me through His Word that calling does not depend on confidence or credentials.

"... 'Not by might nor by power, but by my Spirit,' says the LORD Almighty" (Zechariah 4:6).

"You did not choose me, but I chose you and appointed you so that you might go and bear fruit—fruit that will last ..." (John 15:16).

My own journey has been slow. There were seasons of waiting, wondering, and walking by faith when fruit wasn't visible yet. And yet, through it all, God was weaving a story bigger and more beautiful than anything I could have orchestrated myself. Helping to host my first retreat, and being one of the speakers for a full hour, was a glimpse of God's faithfulness in action.

As *Faithfully Flourishing* began to take shape, it felt natural and necessary to intertwine it with Time Wise Mastery. *Faithfully Flourishing* speaks to identity, calling, and spiritual formation, while Time Wise Mastery provides the practical, lived-out application of those truths in everyday life. One addresses the heart and spirit; the other helps you walk that truth out with clarity, structure, and intention.

Together, they create an experience that doesn't stop at inspiration, but moves toward transformation.

Faithfully Flourishing was born through obedience, not ambition. It grew out of community, prayer, and a deep conviction that our work is an extension of our faith, not separate from it.

He who called me is faithful and will continue the good work He started. And He will do the same for you.

How to Use This Book

This book can be used individually or in a group setting. It is designed as a three-week journey. Through these weeks, you will:

- Be reminded that you were created to create.
- Be challenged to faithfully steward
  your God-given gifts.
- Be commissioned to flourish faithfully, rooted
  in His promises, not the world's pressures.

Take your time as you move through each section. Pray. Reflect. Journal honestly. Allow God to prune what needs pruning, refresh what feels weary, and water what He has planted.

You do not need to move faster. You do not need to have everything figured out. Heaven celebrates faithfulness more than speed. This journey is about rooted growth and surrendered obedience.

This is not a race. This is a relationship.

My prayer is that as you walk through these pages, you will gain clarity, peace, and confidence to steward what God has placed in your hands. I am believing with you for a beautiful harvest that comes from faithful obedience.

You are seen. You are chosen. You are flourishing, one obedient step at a time.

With love and prayers,

Ginger Steg

Embracing Your God-Given Purpose

When I first felt the nudge to step into entrepreneurship, I didn't fully recognize it as a calling. I thought I was simply using the skills God gave me (organizing, helping, and leading), but deep down, there was a stirring I couldn't ignore.

Could this be part of my purpose?

Reading Genesis 1:27–28 opened my eyes:

"So God created mankind in his own image, in the image of God he created them; male and female he created them. God blessed them and said to them, 'Be fruitful and increase in number ...'"

God created me to create, and not just to create for survival but to multiply goodness, impact, and Kingdom purpose through my gifts.

It was very slow going at first. Clients didn't come rushing in. Opportunities didn't explode overnight.

There were long seasons of questioning: "Did I really hear You right, Lord? Was I supposed to build this?"

But even in the slow seasons, God was building me. He was teaching me to work with all my heart, as working for the Lord, not for human masters (Colossians 3:23). He was deepening my faith beyond the circumstances.

Every slow step was actually preparation ground. Every unseen act of obedience mattered more than I realized.

If you're reading this and wondering if your slow start disqualifies you, I want to let you know that it doesn't. God's timelines are different. Your calling is not invalid because it's unfolding slowly. Your assignment still stands because He is the One who called you.

You are created to create. You are chosen to multiply. As you begin this week, remember: Your business, your ideas, and your leadership are sacred ground. You are partnering with the Creator Himself to multiply beauty, goodness, and impact in the world.

Your gifts are on purpose, for a purpose.

This week builds the foundation for walking boldly in your God-given purpose:

- In your identity when you know you are created in God's image to create
- In your preparation when you see slow seasons as sacred building time
- In your obedience when you work as for the Lord, not for human approval
- In your patience when you trust God's timelines over worldly expectations
- In community when you are surrounded by women who champion your calling
- In your assignment when you step forward even before everything is clear

This is a week of realignment, letting go of timelines that don't belong to you and embracing the pace of partnership with God.

This is a week of awareness, recognizing that every unseen act of obedience is preparation ground.

This is a week of courage, choosing to create even when growth feels slow.

This is a week of grounding, anchoring your calling in the unchanging truth that God has appointed you to multiply His goodness.

By the end of Week 1, you will feel:

- More anchored in the truth that you were created to create
- More aware of God's presence in the slow, faithful work
- More certain that your assignment is valid even when growth is gradual
- More equipped to handle seasons of waiting without doubting your calling
- More confident in your ability to steward your gifts with Kingdom purpose

This week will help you become rooted in your identity as a co-creator with God, faithful in the unseen seasons, and steady in the truth that Heaven celebrates your obedience.

Your calling to create is not dependent on speed, scale, or immediate success. You are partnering with the Creator Himself, and He is building something eternal through your faithful "yes."

This is your week to rise grounded, anchored, and confident in the calling God has placed on your life.

Daily Challenge

As you begin Week 1, anchor your heart in these foundational truths. Speak them over yourself daily, letting God's Word shape your identity and strengthen your confidence.

"I praise you because I am fearfully and wonderfully made; your works are wonderful, I know that full well." Psalm 139:14

"For we are God's handiwork, created in Christ Jesus to do good works, which God prepared in advance for us to do." Ephesians 2:10

"being confident of this, that he who began a good work in you will carry it on to completion until the day of Christ Jesus." Philippians 1:6

Choose one verse to memorize this week and write it somewhere you'll see it daily: your planner, your mirror, or your phone lock screen.

YOU ARE CALLED TO CREATE

Wisdom from the Word ————————

"So God created mankind in his own image, in the image of God he created them; male and female he created them. God blessed them and said to them, 'Be fruitful and increase in number; fill the earth and subdue it ...'"
> Genesis 1:27–28

"Whatever you do, work at it with all your heart, as working for the Lord, not for human masters, since you know that you will receive an inheritance from the Lord as a reward. It is the Lord Christ you are serving."
> Colossians 3:23–24

"For we are God's handiwork, created in Christ Jesus to do good works, which God prepared in advance for us to do."
> Ephesians 2:10

ANCHORED IN THE LORD: Flourishing Foundations & Grounded Growth

When God created the heavens and the earth, His work was good, perfect, and full of beauty. Yet even in that perfection, He chose to invite Adam and Eve into a deeper story by placing them into a finished garden that was meant to be cultivated further.

Creation was never meant to be static but designed to be multiplied, cultivated, organized, named, and expanded through partnership with mankind. God's blessing over Adam and Eve extended beyond having families. It was about co-laboring with Him to multiply goodness over the earth. Today, God still calls His daughters into that sacred partnership.

Your business, ideas, leadership, and vision are not random or selfish pursuits but modern-day extensions of Eden's original command: Be fruitful, multiply, influence, and steward. When you create a business that blesses others, solves problems, brings beauty, or restores order, you are fulfilling your Genesis calling.

As a Christian woman in business, you are not just generating revenue. You are expanding the Kingdom. You are not just offering services. You are offering solutions that carry the fingerprint of Heaven. Your business is a piece of Kingdom expansion, an answer to someone's prayer, and a vessel through which God's creativity, excellence, and compassion flow into a broken world.

When you see your work this way, your perspective transforms. Your confidence increases because you realize you're on assignment from Heaven. Your anxiety decreases because you realize the outcomes belong to God. Your creativity flows because you realize the Spirit of the Creator lives in you.

You are not a random collection of gifts, passions, and ideas. You are evidence of the Creator's heart, and your creativity, leadership, innovation, and entrepreneurial spirit are living proof that you carry His image.

Anchor Truth

Genesis 1:27–28 tells us from the beginning that humanity was not simply placed on Earth to survive. We were placed here to create, cultivate, and steward.

Colossians 3:23–24 reminds you that your work is an act of worship. Excellence honors God, and faithfulness is never wasted in His economy.

Ephesians 2:10 teaches us that our work is not random or self-made. We are God's handiwork, intentionally formed by Him, with good works prepared in advance as part of His divine purpose.

Reflection Questions

1. How does it shift my mindset to know that creating, cultivating, and building are part of God's original design for me?

....

....

....

2. Where in my business or life have I unknowingly separated "spiritual" work from "business" work?

....

....

....

3. In what specific areas of my business am I consciously creating for God's glory, not just for gain?

....

....

....

4. What might it look like to invite God even deeper into the daily operations of my business this week?

....

....

....

Time Wise Mastery Activity: Gift & Growth Inventory

Take a moment to list some of your God-given gifts. Then, take inventory of the ways you've multiplied those gifts. In this way, you are stewarding your time and gifts with wisdom and clarity.

My God-Given Gifts

....

....

....

How I've Grown or Used Them in My Business

....

....

....

Pro Tip for Busy Women in Business

Before launching any new project or service, pause and ask, "Whose prayer is my business answering this week?" A Kingdom-focused filter can transform your entire business strategy.

DECLARATION

I am created in the image of the Creator. I am called to multiply goodness, beauty, and Kingdom impact through my work. My business is an extension of my faith, not separate from it. I work as unto the Lord, stewarding the gifts He has placed in my hands. I walk in holy confidence, creative, purposeful, and grounded because I belong to the God who called me to create.

PRAYER

Father God,

Thank You for calling me before I felt qualified. Thank You for placing dreams and ideas in my heart that reflect Your purpose, not my own striving. Today, I acknowledge that my business is not separate from my faith. I invite You into every decision, every step, and every beginning. Help me trust You as I start, even when I cannot see the full picture.

In Jesus' name, Amen.

CLOSING ENCOURAGEMENT

From the very beginning, God designed you to cultivate, create, and steward. Your business is not selfish. It is sacred. It is Kingdom work disguised as daily work. So release the guilt. Release the doubt. Release the lie that what you're building doesn't matter. It does. And your Heavenly Father sees and celebrates it all.

TRADING COMPARISON FOR CALLING

Wisdom from the Word

"Each one should test their own actions. Then they can take pride in themselves alone, without comparing themselves to someone else,"
Galatians 6:4

"Jesus answered, 'If I want him to remain alive until I return, what is that to you? You must follow me.'"
John 21:22

"For God is not a God of disorder but of peace—as in all the congregations of the Lord's people."
1 Corinthians 14:33

ANCHORED IN THE LORD: Flourishing Foundations & Grounded Growth

Comparison is one of the enemy's most effective counterfeit strategies. As Kingdom women in business, we must recognize comparison as a spiritual attack, not just a mindset struggle.

Comparison does more than distract us. It distorts our vision, causing us to see our calling through a cracked lens that filters our purpose through fear, lack, and inadequacy instead of faith, grace, and identity.

It starts subtly: a scroll on Instagram, a glance at someone else's success, a conversation laced with envy masked as admiration. But before you know it, you're questioning if what you're building is even worthy of being on display.

Here's what's really happening in the spirit: The enemy knows he can't take your calling, but he'll try to convince you to abandon it.

He does it by whispering:

- "She's more successful."
- "She started later and got further."
- "Look how polished her brand is."
- "Her client list is bigger."
- "Why even try?"

But those are lies from the pit of hell, designed to delay your obedience, discredit your voice, and deplete your confidence.

When you live in comparison, you live in confusion. Scripture tells us clearly in 1 Corinthians 14:33 that God is not a God of disorder but of peace. Comparison turns your business into a race you were never called to run. It pushes you out of divine rhythm and into worldly striving. It replaces faithfulness with frantic performance.

But God is not asking you to outperform anyone. He's asking you to be faithful to the lane He assigned to you.

Let's break this down with truth:

- **You're not behind.** You're right on time for the divine appointment God has for you. He's not just interested in speed. He's forming strength and depth within you.
- **You're not disqualified.** Your story, your scars, your detours don't disqualify you. They refine you and give your business a testimony.
- **You're not overlooked.** The world may not see your seed seasons, but God does. He sees your

late nights, your obedience, your faithfulness.
And He will reward it in His perfect timing.
- **You're not supposed to do what she's doing.**
You have your own fingerprint, your own grace. The
anointing on her life is not a threat to yours. You
are each a unique celebration of God's creativity.

Imagine a track meet where every runner has a lane. The moment
one runner veers into another's lane, it causes chaos, distraction,
collisions, and disqualifications.

The same is true in the Kingdom. God marked a specific lane for
you, one that fits your story, your strengths, and your season. You
are safest, strongest, and most Spirit-filled when you stay in it.

Veering into someone else's lane costs you momentum. Comparing yourself to others costs you joy. But when you align with God's
path for you, you gain peace, power, and purpose.

You are allowed to celebrate her win without questioning your
worth. You are allowed to admire her journey without abandon-
ing your own. You are allowed to learn from her without losing
your identity.

Her light doesn't dim yours. In the Kingdom, we rise together.

Imagine Jesus whispering this truth over you: "Daughter, I have
not forgotten you. I placed that vision in your heart. I see the
small steps no one else claps for. I am not grading you based on
her progress. I'm growing you according to My perfect plan. You
are right where I need you. Don't run off course now. I have something only you can carry."

Anchor Truth

Galatians 6:4 reminds you to measure your work
against God's calling for your life, not against
someone else's progress. Your growth is between
you and God.

John 21:22 reminds you that Jesus redirects comparison by saying, "What is that to you? You must follow me." Your assignment is to follow Him, not to monitor someone else's journey.

1 Corinthians 14:33 reminds you that God is not a God of confusion. When comparison creates chaos in your mind, it's a sign you've stepped out of God's peace and into the enemy's trap.

Reflection Questions

1. Where in my business or leadership have I allowed comparison to creep in?

....

....

....

2. How has comparison stolen my joy or delayed my obedience?

....

....

....

3. What truth about my identity do I need to declare more boldly?

....

....

....

4. How can I renew my mind and anchor deeper in God's design for my journey?

....

....

....

Time Wise Mastery Activity: Create Your "I Am Called" Declaration

When comparison creeps in, it might look like motivation, but it produces insecurity. It might masquerade as inspiration, but it steals identity. Clarity kicks it out.

Today, write a personalized declaration that anchors you in your unique Kingdom calling.

I am called to _____. I was created to _____. I serve the Kingdom by _____. I let go of _____ and I embrace _____. I run my race with confidence because God has called me by name.

Pro Tip for Busy Women in Business

Before you open an email or social media, take 60 seconds to ask: "What is the one purposeful action God wants me to focus on today?" Starting your day with intention instead of reaction keeps your time aligned with your calling and prevents distraction from stealing your energy.

DECLARATION

I was created with purpose and intention. My worth
is secure in God, not in my output. I move through
my work with clarity, confidence, and peace, trusting
God to multiply what I placed in His hands.

PRAYER

Lord,

Thank You for what You have already entrusted to me. Forgive me for overlooking what is in my hands while wishing for what is not yet mine. Teach me to steward this season with gratitude, faithfulness, and intention. Help me honor You through my work and trust that obedience today prepares me for what is ahead.

In Jesus' name, Amen.

CLOSING ENCOURAGEMENT

There is no competition in the Kingdom, only collaboration and calling.

God isn't watching to see who has more followers or revenue. He is watching to see who stays faithful.

So look up! Lock eyes with the One who called you.

And run your race like it was made just for you—because it was.

PARTNERING WITH GOD'S VISION

Wisdom from the Word

"Then the LORD replied: 'Write down the revelation and make it plain on tablets so that a herald may run with it.'"
        Habakkuk 2:2

"In their hearts humans plan their course, but the LORD establishes their steps."
        Proverbs 16:9

"Unless the LORD builds the house, the builders labor in vain. Unless the LORD watches over the city, the guards stand watch in vain."
        Psalm 127:1

ANCHORED IN THE LORD: Flourishing Foundations & Grounded Growth

The world tells you to dream bigger, push harder, manifest success, and make it happen. But the Spirit says something different: "Come closer. Seek Me first. Surrender the outcome. Let Me show you what I had in mind all along."

When God told Habakkuk to write the vision, it wasn't a motivational speech. It was a divine instruction. God is a God of order, intention, and clarity. But the vision had to come from Him, not from Habakkuk's preferences or fears. God doesn't bless every vision. He blesses what He authors. That's the difference between worldly hustle and Kingdom building. One wears you out. The other lifts you up.

Have you ever found yourself praying over a plan you never invited God into, asking Him to bless something you built without His blueprints? You are not alone. And He's not angry with you. He's inviting you to slow down, to lay your plans on the altar, and to let Him breathe life into what was once self-driven.

Here's the Kingdom key: You don't have to manufacture success. You're called to steward obedience.

When was the last time you let God speak into your vision without rushing to post it, pitch it, or prove it? Your vision doesn't need to be Instagram-worthy. It needs to be anointed. Before you show the world your plans, show them to God. He'll refine, redirect, and restore them in ways you never could imagine.

Signs you're building from pressure, not prayer:

- You feel frantic, not focused
- You measure success by likes, sales, or
  visibility instead of obedience and peace
- You pivot based on trends, not the Holy Spirit
- You're constantly doubting if you're doing enough

But when you build God's way:

- There's clarity in the chaos
- There's peace in the pace
- There's purpose in the process, even when it's slow

God's vision won't lead you into burnout. It will lead you into breakthrough.

Anchor Truth

Habakkuk 2:2 reminds you that God-given vision is clear, purposeful, and meant to be written down so you can run with it. God doesn't give confusion; He gives clarity that guides your steps.

Proverbs 16:9 reminds you that while you can make plans, the LORD establishes your steps. Your role is to plan prayerfully; His role is to direct faithfully.

Psalm 127:1 reminds you that unless the LORD builds the house, the builders labor in vain. Kingdom success comes from building with God, not for God.

REFLECTION QUESTIONS

1. Have I made space for God to speak into my business vision recently?

....

....

....

2. Are there any goals I'm chasing that are rooted in fear, comparison, or pressure?

....

....

....

3. What does it look like to fully surrender my ambition to God's timing and blueprint?

....

....

....

4. How has God uniquely positioned me to solve a problem, meet
   a need, or serve a group of people with love?

....

....

....

Time Wise Mastery Activity: Your Kingdom Vision Map

Use the chart below to prayerfully write out your Kingdom Vision. Don't worry about perfection. Stay focused on presence. Let God speak as you write.

Vision Step	My Response
Who Am I Called to Serve?	
Why Does This Work Matter to Heaven?	
What Fruit Do I Hope to See—Spiritually, Relationally, Financially?	
How Will I Measure Faithfulness?	
What Scripture Anchors This Vision?	

Pro Tip for Busy Women in Business

Before launching into your workday, pause and ask, "God, is this Your vision or mine?" A moment of surrender can redirect your entire strategy.

DECLARATION

Lord, I surrender my plans and pick up Your purpose. I trade hustle for holy. I trade pressure for peace. I trust that the vision You give is greater than the one I could create. I commit to building with Your blueprint. Let my business be a reflection of Your heart, and let it bear eternal fruit. I walk in holy confidence, focused, faithful, and free because I belong to the God who authors my vision.

PRAYER

God,

I bring You my doubts, fears, and uncertainties. When comparison or insecurity tries to creep in, remind me that my calling is unique and intentional. Help me stay focused on You and not distracted by others' journeys. Strengthen my confidence as I walk forward in what You have asked me to build.

In Jesus' name, Amen.

CLOSING ENCOURAGEMENT

You're not building to impress. You're building to impact.

You're not dreaming alone. You're dreaming with the Creator of the universe.

Let Him write the vision. Let Him mark the path. Let Him be your CEO, your CFO, your strategist, and your sustainer.

When God is your architect, legacy becomes your outcome.

OVERCOMING IMPOSTER SYNDROME WITH TRUTH

Wisdom from the Word

"Before I formed you in the womb I knew you, before you were born I set you apart; I appointed you as a prophet to the nations."
   Jeremiah 1:5

"For the Spirit God gave us does not make us timid, but gives us power, love and self-discipline."
   2 Timothy 1:7

"Therefore, if anyone is in Christ, the new creation has come: The old has gone, the new is here!."
   2 Corinthians 5:17

ANCHORED IN THE LORD: Flourishing Foundations & Grounded Growth

Imposter syndrome creeps in when you step into new territory. It holds you back when you try something bold or finally say yes to God's nudge to lead, launch, or level up. It whispers lies like:

- "You're not good enough."
- "You're underqualified."
- "You're pretending, and people will find out."
- "God wouldn't use someone like you."

But those aren't your thoughts. Those are accusations, and your enemy is the accuser.

Scripture is clear: Before you ever doubted your calling, God declared it. He didn't wait for your résumé to be built, your confidence to be strong, or your brand to be polished. He chose you, appointed you, equipped you, and sent you.

When Jeremiah felt inadequate, God didn't tell him to fake it till he made it. He told him, "I knew you. I set you apart. I appointed you." In other words, this has always been My plan.

Most women don't feel like imposters because they're unqualified. They feel like imposters because they're spiritually disconnected from their identity. They're measuring their worth by:

- How many sales came in this week
- Whether their content performed
- If others are ahead of them
- Whether they've done enough

But God never told you to work for worth. He told you to work from your worth.

When you operate from your true identity as a chosen, beloved daughter, you no longer show up to prove yourself. You show up to serve. You show up to steward. You show up because you've already been sent.

Jesus doesn't use perfect people. He uses available ones. Look at His disciples: Peter was hot-headed and impulsive, Thomas was full of doubt, Matthew was a tax collector viewed as a traitor, and Mary Magdalene was healed from torment. None of them were qualified by religious standards, but they were chosen, and they followed.

Imposter syndrome dies the moment you stop listening to your feelings and start anchoring in the facts of God's Word.

Anchor Truth

Jeremiah 1:5 illustrates that before you formed an opinion about yourself, God already knew you, set you apart, and appointed you. Your calling was established before your doubts ever existed.

2 Timothy 1:7 reminds you that the Spirit God gave you doesn't make you timid. God equipped you with power, love, and self-discipline, the very tools you need to walk confidently in your calling.

2 Corinthians 5:17 implores you to embrace that you are a new creation in Christ.

REFLECTION QUESTIONS

1. When have I held back from something God nudged me toward because I didn't feel "ready enough"?

....
....
....

2. How has comparison fueled my imposter syndrome, and who am I constantly measuring myself against?

....
....
....

3. If I truly believed God appointed me before I ever doubted myself, what would I do differently today?

....
....
....

4. What lie about my worthiness shows up most often, and where did I first start believing it?

....

....

....

Time Wise Mastery Activity: The Truth Exchange Chart

Using the examples below, fill out prompts to fight imposter syndrome with truth. Keep it somewhere visible—on your bathroom mirror, your desk, or your phone.

Lie I've Believed	Truth from God's Word
"I'm not good enough."	"I am God's handiwork." (Ephesians 2:10)
"I don't have what it takes."	"His power is made perfect in my weakness." (2 Corinthians 12:9)
"I'm not as far along as I should be."	"He has made everything beautiful in its time." (Ecclesiastes 3:11)
"I'm too new/too late/ too broken."	"The old has gone, the new is here!" (2 Corinthians 5:17)

Now write your own below:

Lie I've Believed	Truth from God's Word

Pro Tip for Busy Women in Business

Before any meeting or presentation, whisper, "I am not an imposter. I am appointed." This simple declaration can shift your confidence from shaky to steady.

DECLARATION

I walk in power, love, and a sound mind. I will no longer
shrink to make others comfortable or wait until I feel "ready."
God has called me, and He goes before me. I lead from
truth, not fear. I rise in confidence, clothed in Christ.

PRAYER

Father,

Thank You for being a God of order, clarity, and peace. Show me where You are inviting me to simplify, align, and refine. Help me release chaos and embrace structure that honors You. I want my work to reflect excellence without striving and discipline without pressure. Lead me with wisdom and grace.

In Jesus' name, Amen.

CLOSING ENCOURAGEMENT

You are not here by accident. You didn't "sneak" into success. You are a masterpiece with a purpose. You were sent by God.

The Lord is not surprised by your position. He prepared it! So walk boldly into rooms you used to feel unqualified for. He's already gone ahead of you.

He's not asking for perfection, He's asking for partnership. Your courage is your yes. Your confidence is Christ.

Abiding Before Advancing

Wisdom from the Word

"I am the vine; you are the branches. If you remain in me and I in you, you will bear much fruit; apart from me you can do nothing."
   John 15:5

"Unless the Lord builds the house, the builders labor in vain. Unless the Lord watches over the city, the guards stand watch in vain."
   Psalm 127:1

"This is what the Sovereign Lord, the Holy One of Israel, says: 'In repentance and rest is your salvation, in quietness and trust is your strength, but you would have none of it.'"
   Isaiah 30:15

ANCHORED IN THE LORD: Flourishing Foundations & Grounded Growth

In business and leadership, we are often taught that momentum equals movement. The faster we go, the more successful we must be. Productivity becomes proof of progress, and rest can feel like falling behind. But God's Kingdom works differently. Fruit does not come from frantic effort. It comes from remaining connected to the source.

Jesus did not say, "Produce fruit and then come to Me." He said, "Remain in Me, and you will bear much fruit." Abiding is not an optional practice for slow seasons. It is the foundation of faithful flourishing. When we remain connected to Christ, our work flows from relationships instead of pressure.

Disconnection rarely happens all at once. It happens subtly.

- Skipping prayer to get a head start on the day.
- Carrying decisions without inviting God into them.
- Measuring success by output instead of obedience.

Before we realize it, we are doing good work without staying rooted in the vine.

Here's what's really happening in the spirit:

The enemy does not need to stop your calling if he can simply exhaust you while you pursue it alone.

And he does it by whispering lies like:

- "If you slow down, you'll fall behind."
- "This all depends on you."
- "You can rest later, after you prove yourself."

But those lies are designed to disconnect you from your source.

When you advance without abiding, your work becomes heavy. Pressure increases. Peace fades. Joy becomes conditional. But when you abide first, your work becomes fruitful. Not because you are doing more, but because God is doing what only He can do through you.

Abiding restores divine rhythm. It replaces urgency with trust. It reminds you that obedience matters more than speed and that fruit grows best when roots go deep.

Today is an invitation to pause, remain, and reconnect. You are not the source of your success. God is. Your role is not to strive harder, but to stay rooted deeper.

Anchor Truth

John 15:5 reminds you that fruit is the result of remaining connected to Christ, not pushing yourself harder. When you stay rooted in Him, growth happens naturally through His strength, not your effort.

Psalm 127:1 anchors you in the truth that success without God's involvement leads to empty labor. When the Lord is the builder, your work carries purpose, peace, and lasting impact.

Isaiah 30:15 reveals that strength is found in rest, trust, and quiet confidence in God. Abiding restores your spiritual rhythm and reminds you that you are sustained by connection, not pressure.

REFLECTION QUESTIONS

1. Where in my business or life have I been advancing without abiding?

....

....

....

2. What does remaining in Christ look like in my daily work rhythm?

....

....

....

3. How might my peace increase if I allowed God to be the source instead of myself?

....

....

....

4. What fruit I am trusting God to produce as I abide?

....

....

....

Time Wise Mastery Activity: The Abiding Anchor

Check in with yourself to identify where hurry has taken root in your life and where abiding needs to grow. Then, list the practices that help you stay spiritually connected.

Where I'm Feeling Rushed or Pressured	Where I'm Being Invited to Pause and Remain in God	What Helps Me Stay Spiritually Connected During My Workday

Pro Tip for Busy Women in Business

Today, choose one intentional pause with God before working. This could be five minutes of prayer before opening your laptop or sitting quietly with Scripture before responding to messages. Let connection come before productivity.

DECLARATION

I remain in Christ, my true source.

I release striving and receive connection.

My fruit flows from intimacy with God, not effort alone.

PRAYER

Lord,

When I feel tired, overwhelmed, or unsure, remind me that You are my strength. Help me release the pressure to prove myself and instead rest in Your approval. Teach me to work from a place of peace, trusting that You are multiplying my efforts in ways I cannot see.

In Jesus' name, Amen.

CLOSING ENCOURAGEMENT

You do not need to rush to be fruitful. Stay connected. Remain rooted. God is faithful to produce what He has promised.

Reflecting on What God Has Revealed

Wisdom from the Word

"He says, 'Be still, and know that I am God; I will be exalted among the nations, I will be exalted in the earth.'"
   Psalm 46:10

"Give careful thought to the paths for your feet and be steadfast in all your ways."
   Proverbs 4:26

"If any of you lacks wisdom, you should ask God, who gives generously to all without finding fault, and it will be given to you."
   James 1:5

ANCHORED IN THE LORD: Flourishing Foundations & Grounded Growth

Stillness is not weakness in the Kingdom. It is wisdom. Yet in business and leadership, stillness is often misunderstood as stagnation. We are conditioned to believe that if we pause too long, we will miss something important. But God does some of His deepest work when we slow down long enough to notice.

Reflection is how revelation becomes rooted. Without it, truth stays surface level. God may speak clearly, but if we rush ahead without reflecting, we risk carrying information instead of wisdom. Reflection allows us to recognize what God has already revealed and how it is meant to shape us.

Reflection does not always come naturally. It often requires intentional space.

- Space to notice where God affirmed you.
- Space to acknowledge where He corrected you.
- Space to recognize where He invited you deeper.

Without reflection, we move forward unchanged.

Here's what's really happening in the spirit:

The enemy cannot silence God's voice, but he will try to crowd it out with noise, urgency, and distraction.

And he does it subtly:

- Filling your schedule so tightly there is no margin to listen.
- Keeping your mind busy replaying what needs to be done next.
- Convincing you that slowing down is unproductive.

But God is not found in the frenzy. He is found in stillness.

When you reflect, clarity replaces confusion. You begin to see patterns instead of pressure. You recognize what is aligned and what needs adjustment. Reflection helps you discern whether your actions are flowing from faith or fear.

God often reveals direction not through loud commands, but through quiet confirmations. When you pause long enough to reflect, you allow His wisdom to settle into your heart and guide your next steps.

Today is an invitation to slow down and pay attention. God has already been speaking this week. Reflection allows you to receive what He has been saying and carry it forward with confidence and peace.

Anchor Truth

Psalm 46:10 reminds you that knowing God comes through stillness, not striving. When you pause, His presence brings clarity that noise can never produce.

Proverbs 4:26 anchors you in intentional awareness. Careful reflection helps you evaluate where you are going and align your steps with wisdom rather than urgency.

James 1:5 reassures you that God gives wisdom generously when you ask. Reflection positions your heart to receive insight that guides your decisions with peace and confidence.

REFLECTION QUESTIONS

1. What moment or conversation this week made me feel most aligned with God's presence?

....

....

....

2. Where did I notice resistance, and what might that resistance be protecting or revealing?

....

....

....

3. If I could distill this week into one sentence of what God was teaching me, what would it be?

....

....

....

4. What truth do I want to carry forward into the days ahead?

....

....

....

Time Wise Mastery Activity: Your Spiritual Reflection Inventory

Take a few minutes to write down and reflect on what God has been showing you this week.

What God Revealed to Me This Week	What Challenged or Stretched Me	What Brought Peace or Confirmation

Pro Tip for Busy Women in Business

Set aside uninterrupted time today to review what stood out to you this week. Write it down. Do not rush to solve or fix anything. Simply notice what God has revealed.

DECLARATION

I slow down to hear God clearly.

I honor stillness as a place of wisdom.

I receive what God has revealed and trust His leading.

PRAYER

God,

I surrender control and timelines to You. Help me trust Your pace and Your process, even when progress feels slow. Give me patience to stay obedient and faith to keep moving forward. I choose to believe that You are faithful to complete the work You have begun in me.

In Jesus' name, Amen.

CLOSING ENCOURAGEMENT

You do not need more information. You need integration. God is speaking. Take time to listen and let His wisdom settle deeply.

RECOMMITTING TO A FAITHFUL PACE

Wisdom from the Word

"but those who hope in the Lord will renew their strength. They will soar on wings like eagles; they will run and not grow weary, they will walk and not be faint."

> Isaiah 40:31

"And we know that in all things God works for the good of those who love him, who have been called according to his purpose."

> Romans 8:28

"… he who began a good work in you will carry it on to completion until the day of Christ Jesus."

> Philippians 1:6

ANCHORED IN THE LORD: Flourishing Foundations & Grounded Growth

Recommitment is not about starting over. It is about realigning your heart with God's pace. As this week comes to a close, God is not asking you to evaluate how much you accomplished. He is inviting you to look at how you walked with Him.

In business and leadership, we often believe that forward progress requires constant motion. Slowing down can feel risky, especially when there is still so much to do. But God is not impressed by speed. He is honored by obedience. A faithful pace sustains what frantic striving eventually breaks.

Recommitment begins with honesty: Honest recognition of where you rushed ahead. Honest acknowledgment of where you carried pressure alone. Honest surrender of expectations God never placed on you.

This kind of honesty is not discouraging. It is freeing.

Here's what's really happening in the spirit:

God is not calling you to do more. He is calling you to walk differently.

And He does it gently:

- By inviting you to trust His timing instead of forcing outcomes.
- By reminding you that He finishes what He starts.
- By offering renewal where you feel weary and worn.

When you recommit to a faithful pace, strength is restored. Anxiety loosens its grip. Direction becomes clearer. You begin to move forward with peace instead of pressure, confidence instead of comparison.

Faithful flourishing is built one obedient step at a time. Not every step will feel significant. Not every season will feel productive. But when your pace is aligned with God, nothing is wasted. He is using every moment to strengthen your roots so you can sustain the fruit that is coming.

Today is an invitation to recommit. To release urgency. To choose trust. To walk into the next week anchored in faith rather than driven by fear.

You are not behind. You are being led. And when you walk at God's pace, you will not grow weary.

Anchor Truth

Isaiah 40:31 reminds you that renewal flows from trusting God, not pushing past your limits. Strength is restored when your hope remains anchored in Him.

Romans 8:28 promises that God is working through every part of your life to bring about good as you walk in love and alignment with His purpose, even when it does not feel good in the moment.

Philippians 1:6 reassures you that God finishes what He begins. You are not responsible for the outcome, only for walking faithfully with Him as He completes the work.

REFLECTION QUESTIONS

1. Where have I been moving faster than God has asked?

....

....

....

2. What does a faithful pace look like in this season of my life and business?

....

....

....

3. Is my current pace fully aligned with God's purpose and plan?

....

....

....

4. What am I recommitting to as I move into Week 2?

....

....

....

Time Wise Mastery Activity:
The Faithful Pace Alignment

Using the reflection questions as prompts, take 5–10 minutes to evaluate your current pace.

Which Areas of My Life or Business Feel Rushed?

Where Is God Asking Me to Slow Down?

What Intentional Adjustments Can I Make for the Coming Week?

Pro Tip for Busy Women in Business

Identify one area where you need to slow down or simplify moving into next week. Write it down and ask God to guide your pace instead of pressure you forward.

DECLARATION

I choose to walk in faithfulness, not urgency.

I release the pressure to rush and trust God's timing.

I move forward aligned with peace, guided by His hand.

PRAYER

Father,

Thank You for walking with me through this week. Thank You for the clarity, conviction, and encouragement You have provided. As I reflect, help me carry these lessons forward with intention. I commit my business, my calling, and my future fully into Your hands. I move forward trusting You completely.

In Jesus' name, Amen.

CLOSING ENCOURAGEMENT

As you prepare to move into Week 2, remember this. You are not behind and you are not late. God is leading you step by step. Carry what He has shown you this week with confidence and trust. He is faithful to establish your path and will continue the good work He has already begun

EMBRACING YOUR GOD-GIVEN PURPOSE

This week marked the beginning of a deeper, stronger, and more anchored walk with God—a walk built on identity, intimacy, and intentionality rather than on hustle, comparison, or pressure.

You have spent the past seven days learning what it truly means to partner with the Creator:

- Confidence rooted in who God created you to be, not who the world says you should become
- Clarity that comes from seeking His vision, not chasing trends
- Freedom from comparison as you embrace your unique, anointed lane
- Authority over imposter syndrome as you stand on the truth of who God says you are
- Peace in the pace as you learn to abide rather than strive
- Strength renewed through stillness and surrender to God's timing

And through each day, one truth has become clearer: Your business is not separate from your faith. It is an extension of it. You are not building alone. You are partnering with the Creator Himself.

You are not the same woman you were seven days ago. You've begun walking differently. You're more aware of God's presence in your work, more grounded in your purpose, more intentional in your decisions, more surrendered to His plan.

Your calling has started to shift from something you question into something you're learning to steward with confidence.

Identity is settling. Comparison is shrinking. Truth is strengthening.

This week, you:

- Reclaimed your identity as a Kingdom entrepreneur: chosen, anointed, and called to create
- Anchored your business in biblical truth, not worldly trends
- Let go of comparison and embraced your God-designed assignment
- Partnered with God's vision over your own ambition
- Replaced imposter syndrome with truth and spiritual authority
- Realigned your business pace and goals with God's rest and rhythm
- Remembered that you are building not for recognition, but for eternal impact

You didn't just learn more about God's heart for your business, you returned to your own.

WHAT YOU'VE LEARNED THIS WEEK

Day 1 — You Were Made to Create

Your creativity, leadership, and entrepreneurial spirit are living proof that you carry God's image. You are partnering with the Creator Himself to multiply goodness in the world.

Day 2 — Trading Comparison for Calling

Your lane is anointed. Stay in it. There is no competition in the Kingdom, only collaboration and calling. Her light doesn't dim yours.

Day 3 — Partnering With God's Vision

God doesn't bless every vision. He blesses what He authors. When God is your architect, legacy becomes your outcome.

Day 4 — Overcoming Imposter Syndrome With Truth

You are not an imposter. You are appointed. Before you ever doubted your calling, God declared it. He knew you, set you apart, and sent you.

Day 5 — The Power of Abiding

Fruit comes not from frantic effort, but from faithful abiding. When you remain connected to the Vine, everything you build flows from intimacy, not just initiative.

Day 6 — Reflect and Recalibrate

Reflection is not wasted time. It's sacred time. When you pause to notice what God is doing, you position yourself to partner with Him more fully in the days ahead.

Day 7 — Recommit and Move Forward

Recommitment is choosing to move forward with what God has spoken. Seed seasons always feel like silence before the harvest, but underground, roots are forming.

REFLECTION FOR THE WEEK

Take a moment today to pause and breathe. Look back over this week and ask yourself:

1. What truth from this week shifted the way I see myself as a woman in business?

....

....

....

2. What area of my business or leadership did I surrender back to God this week?

....

....

....

3. How did I experience God's presence in my work, schedule, or relationships?

....

....

....

4. Where did I feel stretched, and what do I believe God was growing in me through it?

....

....

....

5. What limiting belief, comparison, or fear did I release and lay at the feet of Jesus?

....

....

....

6. What idea, vision, or direction has God started to reveal for my next season?

....

....

....

7. Where am I invited to rest, recharge, and realign before moving forward?

....

....

....

Faithfulness doesn't grow in leaps. It grows in layers. And you have laid a beautiful, solid foundation.

Time Wise Mastery Review: Your Weekly Alignment

Take 20–30 minutes of quiet time to prayerfully answer these check-in questions:

What did I learn this week?

....

....

....

Where did I feel most aligned with God?

....

....

....

What truth am I still wrestling with?

....

....

....

What small win or fruit did I see?

....

....

....

What needs to shift in my mindset, schedule, or systems?

....

....

....

What is God asking me to surrender?

....

....

....

What is God asking me to step into?

....

....

....

Pro Tip for Busy Women in Business

Choose your favorite truth from this week and make it your "confidence anchor" for the next seven days. Put it on your mirror, your phone, or your laptop. Let it steady your spirit every time your confidence wavers.

DECLARATION FOR THE WEEK AHEAD

I am created in the image of the Creator. I am called to multiply goodness, beauty, and Kingdom impact through my work. My business is an extension of my faith. I refuse to measure my journey by someone else's timeline. I surrender my plans and pick up God's purpose. I am appointed. I work as unto the Lord, stewarding the gifts He has placed in my hands. I abide in Him, and from that place of intimacy, I bear fruit that lasts. I am faithfully flourishing by His grace, for His glory.

PRAYER

Father God,

Thank You for meeting me in this first week of reflection and re-alignment. Thank You for reminding me that my calling is intentional and that You are present in every part of my work and life. As I pause to reflect, help me carry forward the clarity, conviction, and peace You have placed in my heart.

I release the need to rush, prove, or operate from pressure. I choose to trust Your timing, Your process, and Your provision. Strengthen my faith as I continue building with obedience, excellence, and purpose. I commit everything I am creating into Your hands, confident that You are guiding each step.

In Jesus' name, Amen.

CLOSING ENCOURAGEMENT

You're not building alone. You're not hustling for validation. You are co-laboring with Heaven. Keep showing up. Keep creating from a place of truth. Keep building what only you can build.

The success of other women doesn't threaten yours. God's vision for you is unique. Your pace is not behind. Your calling is not less than. Your beginning is not insignificant. You were made to create. And every faithful step you take is Kingdom ground. This is just the beginning.

Stewarding What You've Built with Excellence & Order

*A*t some point in your journey, the dream that once stirred excitement in your soul may now feel like a never-ending to-do list.

What started as a sacred whisper, a God-given vision, has slowly gotten tangled in overwhelm, exhaustion, and disorganized days. The creativity that once flowed freely now gets drowned out by client calls, calendar chaos, and a running list of things you didn't get done.

You wonder, *Where did the joy go?* You whisper, "I just need a minute to breathe."

You may simply be at a crossroads. Many faith-filled women entrepreneurs find themselves here, not because they're off track, but because God is inviting them to something deeper: stewardship.

God never asked you to do everything. He asked you to faithfully care for what He's already placed in your hands. Excellence begins not in bigger platforms, but in how you show up right now.

Excellence is not perfection. It's presence. It's intention. It's order born from alignment.

In Genesis, before God filled the earth, He formed it. He brought light to the dark. He separated and structured. He prepared space for what He would then bless.

That's your invitation this week: to bring order where there's been overwhelm, to partner with God in the practical, and to stop running and start reigning right where you are.

This week, you will learn how to steward what God has entrusted to you with wisdom, clarity, and intentionality. Faithful stewardship goes beyond managing tasks and becomes a way of honoring God. It affects the way you handle your time, your resources, your assignments, your systems, your relationships, and your responsibilities.

Faithful stewardship is strengthened when you:

- Steward your vision with clarity
- Steward your assignments with faithfulness
- Steward your time with purpose
- Steward your systems with order
- Steward your business with excellence
- Steward your capacity with wisdom
- Steward your calling with integrity

Stewardship takes practice, but it will shape your entire approach to business and life.

This week will help you:

- Shift from vision to sustainable stewardship
- Evaluate your current assignments
  through a Kingdom lens
- Operate your business with excellence and intentionality
- Address the gaps between calling and capacity
- Build systems that support growth instead of draining you
- Honor what's already in your hands
  before chasing what's next

By the end of Week 2, you will feel more equipped, more grounded, and more in control of the areas God has entrusted to you. You will recognize that stewardship is not about doing more but about faithfully caring for what you already have.

Faithfulness is your fuel. Stewardship is your strategy.

He is not asking you to carry it all. He is asking you to carry it well, with grace, wisdom, and boundaries that protect the beauty of your calling.

When you organize your time, systems, and heart around Him, stewardship stops being overwhelming and becomes an act of worship.

DAILY CHALLENGE

Each morning during Week 2, stand in front of a mirror and speak these truths out loud:

> I am a Kingdom entrepreneur.
>
> I abide in Christ, and I bear fruit from a place of intimacy and identity.
>
> I release performance and receive purpose.
>
> I reject fear and walk in faith.
>
> I am being prepared for impact. I am faithfully flourishing.

Say each truth with boldness, even if you don't feel it yet. Faith grows in the declaration.

FAITHFULNESS OVER FRANTIC GROWTH

Wisdom from the Word ───────────

"Whoever can be trusted with very little can also be trusted with much, and whoever is dishonest with very little will also be dishonest with much."
>   Luke 16:10

"Who dares despise the day of small things ..."
>   Zechariah 4:10

"The plans of the diligent lead to profit as surely as haste leads to poverty."
>   Proverbs 21:5

ANCHORED IN THE LORD: Flourishing Foundations & Grounded Growth

Frantic growth is the counterfeit of faithfulness. It may look like success on the outside, but anxiety often hides on the inside.

In today's business world, there's heavy pressure to scale quickly, expand fast, and prove your value with visible numbers. But the Kingdom of God moves differently. God values roots before fruit, integrity before visibility, and faithfulness over flashiness.

Frantic growth is loud, fast, and externally impressive, but it can also be spiritually hollow. It might sparkle on the surface with a viral reel, a sold-out launch, a packed calendar, or a six-figure announcement. But if you peel back the layers, frantic growth often conceals burnout, insecurity, scarcity-driven decisions, and misaligned motives.

Frantic growth asks, "How much can I get done today to prove I'm enough?" Faithful growth asks, "What has God actually asked me to do today?"

In the world of business, you're bombarded with slogans like "rise and grind," "scale fast or fall behind," "sleep when you're dead," and "don't stop until you're proud." But the Kingdom whispers something different:

- "Be still and know that I am God."
- "Apart from Me, you can do nothing."
- "He has made everything beautiful in its time."
- "Those who wait upon the Lord
  shall renew their strength."

God cannot be rushed. Beyond that, He is more interested in who you become on the way to your destination than merely getting there.

When God entrusts you with a business, He's not just giving you a platform. He's giving you a process. In that process, He is far more focused on your roots than your reach. Fruit without roots will rot. Influence without integrity will crumble. Sales without surrender will leave you striving.

The world celebrates numbers. Heaven celebrates names. The world rewards speed, but Heaven rewards obedience. Faithfulness won't always trend, but it will transform you, your business, your clients, and your legacy.

God doesn't just bless big moves. He blesses obedient steps: one act of faith at a time, one customer served with love, one product built in prayer, one meeting held with integrity, one email sent with excellence.

When you choose faithfulness over franticness, you stop living for the applause of others and start building for the approval of God. You silence the noise of hustle culture and enter the peace of Kingdom culture.

Faithful growth often looks unseen by the crowd, unimpressive to the world, and unshared on social media. But in the spiritual realm, foundational work matters. God isn't just preparing your business. He's preparing you, building strength in your systems, character in your leadership, and wisdom in your decision-making. When the blessings come, He wants you strong enough to sustain them.

Sometimes, we chase growth because we're afraid we'll be forgotten if we don't move fast. But fast success is not always favored success. God's timing is not our timing. Remember, He created the seasons. When you rush what God is trying to root, you risk building something that won't last.

Faithful growth looks like showing up with excellence when no one's watching, repeating the same good habit until it becomes fruit-bearing, saying no to shiny distractions to protect what matters most, and allowing God to prune, refine, and even pause you when necessary.

Sometimes, the most spiritual thing you can do for your business is to slow down and ask: "God, is this step Spirit-led or fear-fueled?"

Anchor Truth

Luke 16:10 reminds you that God watches how you manage the small things before He multiplies them. Faithfulness matters at every level.

Zechariah 4:10 shows that God rejoices in small beginnings. Your current season is not insignificant. It's sacred.

Proverbs 21:5 teaches that diligent planning leads to profit, but hasty decisions lead to loss. Wisdom takes time.

REFLECTION QUESTIONS

1. Where am I tempted to pursue growth out of fear, comparison, or pressure?

....

....

....

2. What small responsibility has God asked me to steward that I've been overlooking?

....

....

....

3. Have I been rushing ahead of God's pace? What is He inviting me to do instead?

....

....

....

4. What would it look like to trade hustle for holy diligence?

....

....

....

Time Wise Mastery Activity: The Faithfulness Filter

Use this filter before taking action in your business this week. Write your answers down and return to them whenever you feel the urge to "push harder" instead of "grow wiser."

Decision or Opportunity	Why Do I Want to Do This?	Is This Aligned With My Current Assignment?

Pro Tip for Busy Women in Business

Before adding anything new to your business this week, pause and ask: "Is God asking me to add this, or is pressure pushing me to prove something?" Write down the answer and let it guide your next step.

DECLARATION

I choose to grow at God's pace. I will not rush what He is rooting. I honor my small beginnings, my quiet progress, and my hidden seasons. I trade frantic hustle for holy stewardship. I am being strengthened in the secret place so I can sustain the harvest when it comes. I will be faithful, and God will be glorified.

PRAYER

Father God,

Thank You for trusting me with what I am building. Help me see my business as a responsibility and an opportunity to honor You. Teach me to steward my time, energy, and resources with wisdom and care. I want to be faithful with what You have already given me.

In Jesus' name, Amen.

CLOSING ENCOURAGEMENT

You are not late. You are not behind. You are being built from the inside out for impact that lasts. God is not impressed by speed, but He rejoices in faithfulness. Keep showing up. Keep stewarding what you've been given. Because in the Kingdom, small beginnings are sacred, and obedience is always the first step toward overflow.

Order Is a Form of Worship

Wisdom from the Word

"For God is not a God of disorder but of peace ..."
   1 Corinthians 14:33

"In the beginning God created the heavens and the earth ..."
   Genesis 1:1–2

"She watches over the affairs of her household and does not eat the bread of idleness."
   Proverbs 31:27

ANCHORED IN THE LORD: Flourishing Foundations & Grounded Growth

Sometimes, the juggle is overwhelming. The orders, the emails, the social media content, the laundry, the team questions, the calendar pings, the forgotten grocery list. It can feel like you're holding too many pieces of a puzzle you don't have time to finish.

We've all said it:

- "It's just a busy season."
- "I'll get organized next month."
- "Everything feels like it's on fire."

We're all busy. But we don't need to carry it all without support, especially without spiritual order. God isn't just the Creator of your calling. He's the Organizer of your overflow.

You don't have to choose between holy and hustle. There is a rhythm to the Kingdom that is not chaotic, not scattered, and not defined by exhaustion or survival mode.

In Genesis, before God ever filled the earth with goodness, He first brought order. He separated light from dark, water from land, time into day and night. God didn't rush into productivity. He prepared the space, and He's calling you to do the same.

You don't need a productivity hack. You need Holy Spirit partnership. And it starts with inviting Him into the details: your calendar, your inbox, your client workflows, your morning routine, even your meal prep. He's not just in your big vision. He's in your Monday morning mess, too.

Let's slow down for a moment. Take a breath. If your calendar feels like a battlefield, if your desk is buried beneath unfinished lists, if your mind is constantly bouncing among tabs, texts, and tasks, you are not failing. You're functioning in survival mode. That's not where God wants you to stay, though. Chaos is a danger zone. It doesn't just create stress, it silences clarity.

The longer we stay in clutter, internally or externally, the harder it becomes to hear God's whisper.

We've been taught to normalize the chaos:

- "Business just looks like this."
- "I'll rest after this launch."
- "One day I'll have a better system."

But God is saying:

- "Daughter, I have more for you than this."
- "Come out of the swirl and step into My rhythm."
- "Let Me order your steps and lighten your load."

Order is not about color-coded calendars or picture-perfect shelves, though we love a good planner. Order is about alignment. When things are in order, your life has flow, not the kind of flow the world defines where everything is perfectly balanced, but the kind where your priorities reflect your purpose, your decisions reflect your values, and your schedule reflects your season. In other words, you live like your life belongs to God.

Let's go back to the beginning. In Genesis, the earth was formless and void. It was dark. The first thing God did wasn't to fill it with beauty. He first spoke light into it, and then He structured it. He created boundaries between sky and sea. He designated time: morning and evening. He assigned rhythms: work then rest, seed time then harvest.

Even in the Garden, there was order before overflow. And when sin entered the world, disorder, disruption, and confusion followed. But through Jesus, we have access to something better: peace, alignment, and holy rhythm.

When we live in alignment with God's design, we are reclaiming the original order of creation. That's not just smart. It's sacred.

When you're constantly overwhelmed, you don't have time to dream. When your mind is cluttered, you forget to pray. When your days are reactive, you end up working from pressure, not from purpose, and what was once your calling begins to feel like a burden.

But it doesn't have to stay that way. The same Spirit that hovered over the chaos of the deep now hovers over your days, ready to help you build what's both beautiful and sustainable.

You don't need to be a perfectionist. You need to be a partner with the Holy Spirit. Order makes space for intimacy with God, and intimacy with God makes space for impact.

This isn't just about cleaning your inbox or updating your systems. This is about preparing a place for God to dwell in your business, your home, your heart. You're not creating order just so your life feels easier. You're creating order so that your life becomes a testimony.

When other women look at how you lead, how you protect your time, how you operate with peace, how you show up without burning out, they'll ask, "How are you doing all of this and still smiling?"

And you'll say: Because I surrendered my chaos to a God of order. Because I stopped letting the world set my pace. Because I learned that structure isn't controlling. It's freeing. Because I'm not building alone. I'm building with Him.

Anchor Truth

1 Corinthians 14:33 reminds you that God is a God of peace, not disorder. When your life reflects order, it reflects His character.

Genesis 1:1–2 shows that God brought structure before He brought abundance. Preparation creates space for blessing.

Proverbs 31:27 teaches that a wise woman watches over her household and doesn't eat the bread of idleness. Stewardship requires intentionality.

REFLECTION QUESTIONS

1. What area of my business or life feels the most chaotic right now?

....

....

....

2. What is one small space, digital or physical, that I could bring order to this week?

....

....

....

3. How would it change my heart if I saw organizing as worship
   instead of just another chore?

....

....

....

Time Wise Mastery Activity:
One Space, One Step

Choose one area of your life or business to bring into alignment this
week, and declare why it matters. You don't have to post about it or
make it pretty. You just need to start.

Area to Organize or Simplify	Why It Matters to Me and My Calling	One Step I'll Take This Week

Pro Tip for Busy Women in Business

Pick one recurring task that drains your energy and create a simple system for it this week. It could be client onboarding, invoic-
ing, or even meal planning. One small system can free up hours
of mental energy.

DECLARATION

God is not the author of chaos. He's the Creator of peace.
I release the lie that busy means important. I embrace
order as an act of worship. My space, time, and business
will reflect the beauty of Heaven. I steward what I've
been given with intention, grace, and excellence.

PRAYER

Lord,

Show me where You are inviting me to bring more order and clarity. Reveal any areas where distraction, overwhelm, or avoidance have taken root. Help me approach my work with intention and peace, knowing You are a God of order. Guide my steps today with discernment.

In Jesus' name, Amen.

CLOSING ENCOURAGEMENT

You don't need to do it all to be worthy. You don't need to fix it all overnight. And you don't need to feel shame about where things are right now. You just need to start faithfully, gently, with God. Let's link arms this week as sisters in business and in faith, and walk out this truth together: When we bring order into our world, we are inviting God to dwell more fully. Our work is a form of worship that will bear eternal fruit.

BOUNDARIES PROTECT THE BLESSING

Wisdom from the Word

"Above all else, guard your heart, for everything you do flows from it."
> Proverbs 4:23

"There is a time for everything, and a season for every activity under the heavens."
> Ecclesiastes 3:1

"Very early in the morning, while it was still dark, Jesus got up, left the house and went off to a solitary place, where he prayed. Simon and his companions went to look for him, and when they found him, they exclaimed: 'Everyone is looking for you!' Jesus replied, 'Let us go somewhere else—to the nearby villages—so I can preach there also. That is why I have come.'"
> Mark 1:35–38

ANCHORED IN THE LORD: Flourishing Foundations & Grounded Growth

Have you ever laid in bed at night, body aching, brain still buzzing, soul completely drained, all because you couldn't say no? No to that last-minute meeting, to the extended deadline, to the client who constantly texts after hours, to the social event you didn't even want to attend, to the fear that if you slow down, it'll all fall apart.

If that hits home, you're not alone. So many of us were raised with the idea that good Christian women should always say yes, that serving others means being endlessly available, that boundaries are barriers, and that protecting your peace is selfish.

But Scripture shows us repeatedly: boundaries are not selfish. They are sacred.

Even Jesus had boundaries. Let that sink in. The Son of God, the One with all power and all compassion, still said no. Still withdrew. Still rested. Still chose silence over proving. Still walked away from need to stay connected to purpose.

In Mark 1, Jesus healed crowds and cast out demons. The whole town came looking for Him. And what did He do the next morning? He didn't run straight into another miracle. He went to a quiet place. Alone. With the Father.

In Mark 1:38, when the disciples came and said, "Everyone is looking for You!" He didn't rush back to the crowds. He said, "Let us go somewhere else, that is why I have come." Even Jesus knew when to walk away from what was good to stay aligned with what was God.

Every time you say yes, you're giving away energy, time, presence, and focus. Your yes is powerful, and that means it needs to be protected.

You weren't created to manage 30 things at once, to be everything to everyone, to fill everyone's cup while yours stays empty, or to serve so hard that you forget how to simply be. Quite the opposite. Loving yourself first enables you to serve others well.

Boundaries are how you honor your capacity. They don't mean you're saying no to love or service. They mean you're saying yes to longevity, because the blessing God gave you (your business, your family, your gifts) needs to be protected.

Walls keep everything out. Boundaries let in what is healthy, holy, and aligned, and gently close the door on what isn't.

Boundaries might look like a firm stop time in your workday, turning off notifications during family dinner, saying not right now to a good idea so you can honor your current assignments, letting clients know your response time with grace and clarity, or carving out quiet time in the morning, even if your to-do list is exploding.

And maybe most of all, boundaries with yourself: saying no to overextending, to comparison that steals your peace, and to guilt that pushes you into proving.

You don't have to say yes to everything just because you can. You are not God. And He never asked you to be.

Faithful flourishing begins where margin meets mission.

We are carrying dreams, raising families, leading businesses, serving clients, discipling others, and trying to keep dinner from burning. And still, we're trying to do it all with joy and grace.

But you can't pour from an empty spirit. You can't hear from God in constant noise. You can't carry your blessing without protecting your boundaries.

Jesus didn't rush. Jesus didn't say yes to every need. Jesus didn't run on burnout. He walked in peace, power, and margin. That's your invitation too.

You don't need to work harder. You need to be wiser. You don't need to do more. You need to do what matters most, with intentionality and God's covering.

The assignment God gave you wasn't meant to crush you. It was meant to partner with you. But you'll never carry it well without building healthy limits around it.

So today, ask yourself: "What is draining me right now that doesn't align with my assignment?" "Where do I need to pull back so I can pour deeper?" "What boundary is God asking me to set, even if it feels uncomfortable at first?"

Peace doesn't just happen. It's protected.

Anchor Truth

Proverbs 4:23 reminds you to guard your heart, for everything flows from it. Boundaries protect what matters most.

Ecclesiastes 3:1 teaches that there is a time for everything. Not everything needs to happen right now, and that's okay.

Mark 1:35–38 shows that even Jesus withdrew, rested, and set boundaries. If He needed margin, so do you.

REFLECTION QUESTIONS

1. Where in my life or business do I feel stretched too thin or constantly overwhelmed?

....

....

....

2. What am I saying yes to that God never asked me to carry?

....

....

....

3. What boundary have I been afraid to set because of fear, guilt, or people-pleasing?

....

....

....

4. How might setting a new boundary actually increase my impact and intimacy with God?

....

....

....

Time Wise Mastery Activity: Boundary Reset Map

Use this space to prayerfully identify and design healthy, Spirit-led boundaries in key areas of your life and business. For example, in the area of "Time," the boundary you may need is "No work calls after 6 p.m." Why it matters? "To protect my time and my energy."

Area	Boundary I Need	Why It Matters
Time		
Spiritual Life		
Social Media		
Personal Space		

Pro Tip for Busy Women in Business

Set one non-negotiable boundary this week and communicate it clearly. It could be your work hours, response time, or a specific day off. Practice saying it without apologizing or over-explaining.

DECLARATION

I am not called to carry everything. I am called to steward what God gave me with wisdom. I set boundaries not out of fear, but out of faith. I choose to protect the peace, the calling, and the people God has entrusted to me. My no is not rejection. It is redirection. My yes is sacred, and I give it wisely.

PRAYER

God,

Thank You for reminding me that excellence honors You. Help me work with integrity, consistency, and care, even in the small and unseen tasks. Remove the pressure to do everything at once and teach me to focus on what matters most today.

In Jesus' name, Amen.

CLOSING ENCOURAGEMENT

You don't need to earn your worth by being endlessly available. You are already chosen. Already enough. Already called. Your boundaries are not pushing people away. They're pulling God in. They're creating space for you to rest, to breathe, and to hear from Him again.

REST IS A STRATEGY, NOT A REWARD

Wisdom from the Word

"Remember the Sabbath day by keeping it holy. Six days you shall labor and do all your work, but the seventh day is a sabbath to the LORD your God. On it you shall not do any work, neither you, nor your son or daughter, nor your male or female servant, nor your animals, nor any foreigner residing in your towns."

Exodus 20:8–10

"Come to me, all you who are weary and burdened, and I will give you rest. Take my yoke upon you and learn from me, for I am gentle and humble in heart, and you will find rest for your souls. For my yoke is easy and my burden is light."

Matthew 11:28–30

"By the seventh day God had finished the work he had been doing; so on the seventh day he rested from all his work. Then God blessed the seventh day and made it holy, because on it he rested from all the work of creating that he had done."

Genesis 2:2–3

ANCHORED IN THE LORD: Flourishing Foundations & Grounded Growth

Before we go any further, I invite you to take a deep breath. Let your shoulders drop. Let your jaw unclench. Let your chest expand. Now breathe out slowly.

Because we're about to talk about something that may be unfamiliar, uncomfortable, and completely essential: rest. Not as a luxury. Not as a backup plan. Not as something you'll finally allow yourself once you've done enough, earned enough, cleaned enough, or succeeded enough, but as a command from God and a gift for your weary soul.

The world says, "Hustle harder." God says, "Come and rest."

Some of us don't know how to stop. We feel guilty when we do. We associate rest with laziness. We're afraid that if we pause, everything will fall apart. We don't rest. We crash. We don't Sabbath. We scroll. We don't slow down. We just numb out.

But that's not God's design for you. That's survival. You weren't made to just get by. You were made to thrive.

In Genesis, after six days of creation, God rested. Not because He was worn out, but because He was modeling the rhythm of life: work, create, tend, then rest. He didn't suggest it. He commands it.

He knows we can't produce from a dry well. He knows the soil of our soul needs regular replenishment. He knows we're fragile beings and that rest is necessary for our souls.

In a culture that worships performance, rest is rebellion. It's saying:

- "I trust God more than I trust my grind."
- "I believe God can do more with my six days than I can with seven."
- "I don't need to earn my value. I already have it in Christ."

Rest is how we recalibrate. Rest is how we return. Rest is how we hear again. When you rest, you're not falling behind. You're falling into alignment.

Rest isn't just naps and spa days, although those are wonderful. Rest can look like logging off at 5 p.m. even when your inbox is full, spending quiet time with God before checking your phone, taking a Sunday to worship, read, nap, and do nothing productive. Rest looks like laughing over dinner without talking business, turning your phone off for 24 hours and letting the world wait, or saying no to taking on one more thing so you can say yes to your health.

Rest isn't an escape. It's equipment. It arms you with clarity, creativity, and connection again.

The invitation of Jesus is clear: "Come to Me, all who are weary."

He doesn't say:

- "Come to Me after you've cleaned up."
- "Come to Me when you've earned it."
- "Come to Me after your inbox is empty."

He says, "Come now. Come tired. Come tangled. Come undone."

Because rest doesn't start when the work is done. Rest is where the real work begins: the internal work, the heart work, the healing.

Anchor Truth

Exodus 20:8–10 reminds you that rest is commanded, not suggested. God instituted the Sabbath because He knows you need it.

Matthew 11:28–30 shows that Jesus invites the weary to come to Him for rest. You don't have to earn it. You're already invited.

Genesis 2:2–3 teaches that God Himself rested after creation and blessed the seventh day. If God rested, so should you.

REFLECTION QUESTIONS

1. Do I feel guilty when I rest? Why?

....

....

....

2. Where have I been pushing beyond my limits, and what is it costing me emotionally, spiritually, or physically?

....

....

....

3. What does rest look like for me in this season, and what practical step can I take to protect it?

....

....

....

4. What might God be trying to say to me that I'm too busy to hear?

....

....

....

Time Wise Mastery Activity: Rhythms of Rest Map

Identify what rest means for you in different areas of your life, and how you'll begin to protect it. Here are some examples:

Area of Life	What Rest Looks Like Here	How I'll Practice It Weekly
Spiritual Life	Worship without multitasking	Quiet time with no phone distractions
Body & Health	A full night of sleep/slowing down workouts	Unplug by 8 p.m. 3 nights/week
Relationships	Laughing, no business talk	Tech-free dinner once a week
Business Boundaries	No email on Sundays	Protect my Sabbath no matter what

Pro Tip for Busy Women in Business

Block off one full day each week as a Sabbath rest day. No emails, no client calls, no content creation. Protect it fiercely and watch how it transforms your clarity and creativity the rest of the week.

DECLARATION

Rest is not something I earn. It's something I receive. I choose to step out of hustle and into holiness. I lay down the lie that my value is in my performance. I will not run on empty. I will refuel with God. I rest not to be lazy, but to be led. I make space for peace, knowing God never stops working, even when I do.

PRAYER

Father,

I invite You into my systems, routines, and daily decisions. Show me what needs to be refined, simplified, or strengthened. Help me steward my business in a way that supports peace, growth, and sustainability. I trust You to lead me with wisdom.

In Jesus' name, Amen.

CLOSING ENCOURAGEMENT

Your Father in Heaven isn't asking you to hustle harder. He's asking you to trust deeper. You don't have to earn rest. Jesus already earned it for you. You're not lazy for needing a break. You're human, and holy. Rest isn't something you'll get to one day. Rest is a strategy for today. So go ahead. Close the laptop. Leave the dishes. Silence the noise. Lay your head down. And know that while you rest, He still reigns.

RESIST WORDLY PERFECTION & EMBRACE EXCELLENCE

Wisdom from the Word ─────────

"He has made everything beautiful in its time. He has also set eternity in the human heart; yet no one can fathom what God has done from beginning to end."

Ecclesiastes 3:11

"But be very careful to keep the commandment and the law that Moses the servant of the Lord gave you: to love the Lord your God, to walk in obedience to him, to keep his commands, to hold fast to him and to serve him with all your heart and with all your soul."

Joshua 22:5

"Be perfect, therefore, as your heavenly Father is perfect."

Matthew 5:48

ANCHORED IN THE LORD: Flourishing Foundations & Grounded Growth

We wear perfectionism like a badge, but it's breaking us. We're constantly editing, constantly second-guessing, constantly thinking, *I could've done more. I should've done better. I don't want to mess this up.*

We delay launches. We rewrite captions. We redo designs that were already good enough. We lose sleep replaying conversations in our heads. We feel that if something isn't perfect, we're not worthy of calling it done. And deep down, we equate perfection with worth, excellence with applause, and success with flawlessness.

God never called you to be perfect. He calls you to be present, obedient, and excellent.

Perfectionism is all about performance, pressure, and self. Excellence is about purpose, presence, and surrender.

Perfection asks, "Will they approve of this?" Excellence asks, "Is this honoring to God?"

Perfection leads to exhaustion, anxiety, and delay. Excellence leads to confidence, peace, and completion. Perfection says, "Do more, be more, prove more." God says, "Do it with Me, and I will multiply it."

Let's look at Jesus. He did everything with purpose, with compassion, with excellence, but He didn't worry about optics. He healed people in unconventional ways. He left crowds still in need. He overturned tables in the temple. He chose disciples who were unpolished, unqualified, and unknown. He didn't try to impress. He came to impact. And when it came to His assignment, He didn't delay for perfection. He fulfilled it with love and obedience.

Excellence looks like putting thought into your work but not idolizing it, showing up prepared but not paralyzed, delivering value (not just chasing validation), creating from rest (not from fear), launching when God says go (not when it feels flawless), and understanding that your best, done with God, is powerful and more than enough.

Some of the most impactful things you do will be slightly messy, not fully polished, not immediately applauded, maybe even misunderstood. But if it's done with love, intention, and faith, it matters. It carries His presence. It carries His purpose. It carries power.

God doesn't anoint your perfection. He anoints your surrender. So stop waiting to feel ready enough. If He called you, you're ready. If He gave you the idea, He will give you the grace to complete it.

Anchor Truth

Ecclesiastes 3:11 reminds you that the God of eternity is not asking for perfection, but faithful excellence over a timeline bigger than you can see.

Joshua 22:5 emphasizes that biblical excellence is about wholehearted devotion, staying close to God, walking faithfully in obedience, and serving Him with sincerity.

Matthew 5:48 calls you to be perfect as your heavenly Father is perfect, but this is about spiritual maturity and wholeness, not earthly perfection.

REFLECTION QUESTIONS

1. Where in my life or business am I striving for perfection rather than showing up in faith?

....

....

....

2. What assignment am I delaying because I fear it won't be good enough?

....

....

....

3. What does excellence mean to me in this season, and how can I pursue it without getting trapped in pressure?

....

....

....

Time Wise Mastery Activity: The Faithful Excellence Step

What project, post, product, or offer have you been waiting to launch because it didn't feel ready enough? Name it. Pray over it. Take one action toward releasing it in excellence, not perfection.

What I've Been Waiting to Launch	Why It Matters to Me and My Calling	One Step I'll Take This Week

Pro Tip for Busy Women in Business

Give yourself a "launch date" for something you've been perfecting. Set a deadline, do your best work in the time you have, and release it, trusting God to multiply your faithful obedience.

DECLARATION

I release the lie that I need to be perfect. I embrace progress, obedience, and surrender. I choose excellence, not to impress, but to honor God. My work doesn't have to be flawless to be fruitful. I am anointed, equipped, and ready, even with my imperfections. I will no longer delay what God has called me to release.

PRAYER

Lord,

When I feel overwhelmed or uncertain, remind me that I do not carry this alone. Help me release comparison and remain focused on the assignment You have given me. Teach me to lead and build from a place of trust and obedience.

In Jesus' name, Amen.

CLOSING ENCOURAGEMENT

Your imperfection does not disqualify your impact. Your unfinished edges don't scare God. They invite Him. Excellence isn't about perfection. It's about being present, prepared, and planted in purpose. So go create. Go serve. Go launch. Go speak. Go build. Not because you've perfected it, but because God is in it. And that will always be more than enough.

PURPOSE OVER PRESSURE

Wisdom from the Word

"for each one should carry their own load."
     Galatians 6:5

"'Come to me, all you who are weary and burdened, and I will give you rest. Take my yoke upon you and learn from me, for I am gentle and humble in heart, and you will find rest for your souls. For my yoke is easy and my burden is light."
     Matthew 11:30

"Cast your cares on the LORD and he will sustain you; he will never let the righteous be shaken."
     Psalm 55:22

ANCHORED IN THE LORD: Flourishing Foundations & Grounded Growth

Let's talk about pressure, that silent weight that creeps in, morning after morning. The pressure to grow. The pressure to post. The pressure to scale. To reply faster. To be more present. To keep it all afloat while trying not to fall apart.

You wake up already feeling behind. You scroll and compare. You smile and serve. You give and go. You tell yourself, "I just need to get through this week."

But deep down, something aches. Because this can't be what Kingdom purpose feels like.

Purpose was never meant to suffocate you. Pressure was.

Pressure is a thief. It steals your peace. It dulls your clarity. It makes you reactive instead of rooted. It drives you to perform instead of pause. It convinces you that everything is urgent, even when it's not important. And the longer you operate from pressure, the more disconnected you become from the Person who assigned your purpose in the first place.

God didn't call you to chase metrics. He called you to make a mark. He's not impressed by how much you carry. He's glorified when you carry what's yours and leave the rest to Him.

Pressure says, "It all depends on me." Purpose says, "It all begins with God."

Pressure says, "Don't slow down or you'll lose momentum." Purpose says, "Come away with Me, and I'll renew your strength."

Pressure says, "You need to do more to keep up." Purpose says, "You're already chosen. Just walk with Me."

Jesus was never in a hurry. Have you noticed that? He was never frantic, never rushing from task to task, never fueled by fear of falling behind.

He knew His purpose. And because of that, He could pause. He could walk slowly through the crowd. He could heal one person and not feel guilty about the ones He hadn't reached yet. He trusted the timing of His Father more than the demands of people. And that's your invitation too.

Purpose brings peace, not because it's always easy, but because it's aligned.

When you're walking in purpose, you know what's yours to carry and what isn't. You stop saying yes out of fear and start saying yes out of faith. You measure success by obedience, not by speed or recognition.

Purpose is what gives your business a heartbeat. Purpose helps you serve from the center of who God made you to be.

Anchor Truth

Galatians 6:5 reminds you that each person should carry their own load. You're not responsible for carrying what God never assigned to you.

Matthew 11:30 are Jesus' words to his disciples, instructing them that through Him, they will find rest for their souls. For them and for you, His yoke is easy and his burden is light.

Psalm 55:22 invites you to cast your cares on the Lord. He will sustain you. You don't have to carry it all alone.

REFLECTION QUESTIONS

1. Where have I said yes to something that is not mine to carry?

....

....

....

2. If I released the pressure to keep up, what new rhythm would I step into?

....

....

....

3. What would it feel like to let God reset the pace of my life and business?

....

....

....

4. What do I know God has asked me to focus on in this season, and what do I need to release?

....

....

....

Time Wise Mastery Activity: Purpose Alignment Check

Use this chart to identify what you're carrying and whether it's led by purpose or fueled by pressure. For example, it might be a weekly newsletter. If it aligns with your calling, ask yourself if you need to continue to create it or if it's time to delegate it. If the responsibility doesn't align, God might be asking you to redefine it, pause it indefinitely, or let it go.

Task/ Responsibility	Does This Align with My Purpose (Yes/No)	What God Might Be Asking Me to Do with It

Pro Tip for Busy Women in Business

List every commitment on your calendar for the next month. For each one, ask: "Did God ask me to do this, or did I say yes out of pressure?" Release what doesn't align with your current assignment.

DECLARATION

I release the pressure to perform. I choose to walk in peace and purpose. I don't have to do it all. I just have to do what God has asked of me. I'm not behind. I'm right where God has me. I walk with intention, not anxiety. I trust God to carry what I was never meant to hold.

PRAYER

God,

Thank You for being patient with me as I learn and grow. Help me extend that same patience to myself. Show me how to steward my energy and rest wisely so I can remain grounded and present in the work You have called me to do.

In Jesus' name, Amen.

CLOSING ENCOURAGEMENT

God didn't ask you to run someone else's race. He didn't ask you to chase every trend. He didn't call you to live exhausted in the name of ambition. You were created for impact, not impressing. You were designed for purpose, not pressure. So take a deep breath. Turn down the noise. Let go of the weight that isn't yours. And walk forward, light, clear, and confident, knowing that what God assigns, He also anoints.

COMMUNITY IS YOUR COVERING

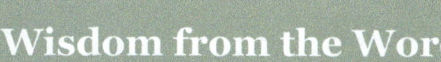

Wisdom from the Word

"Two are better than one, because they have a good return for their labor: If either of them falls down, one can help the other up. But pity anyone who falls and has no one to help them up."
> Ecclesiastes 4:9–10

"Carry each other's burdens, and in this way you will fulfill the law of Christ."
> Galatians 6:2

"And let us consider how we may spur one another on toward love and good deeds, not giving up meeting together, as some are in the habit of doing, but encouraging one another—and all the more as you see the Day approaching."
> Hebrews 10:24–25

ANCHORED IN THE LORD: Flourishing Foundations & Grounded Growth

Entrepreneurship can be lonely. You're the one making the decisions. You're the one who keeps the vision alive. You're the one to whom others turn for encouragement, leadership, or answers.

And some days, the weight of it all feels quiet and heavy. You smile, you lead, you build. But inside, you're whispering, "Is anyone really walking with me?" "Does anyone truly see me?" "If I fall apart, who's catching me?"

Please hear this today: God never meant for you to build your business, or your life, in isolation. You were created for connection. You were wired for community.

In the world, we're taught to prove we can do it alone: be self-made, pull yourself up, don't ask for help, don't show weakness. But in the Kingdom, strength looks different.

Strength is saying "I can't do this without my sisters." Strength is letting others speak life when you can't find the words. Strength is asking for help without shame. Community isn't weakness. It's covering.

You need sisters who will pray over your business when you feel spiritually dry, remind you who you are when you forget, call out your gifts when you doubt yourself, challenge you with love when you start drifting off course, celebrate you when you win (and mean it), and sit with you when you're in the messy middle and say, "Me too."

Because we weren't meant to just network. We were meant to link arms in Kingdom work.

If the enemy can isolate you, he can weaken your resolve, confuse your calling, silence your voice, and steal your joy. But when you're surrounded by Spirit-led women who see you, pray for you, and pour into you, you become a force. Because you stop carrying everything alone. You start walking in rhythm with the Body of Christ.

Community doesn't always show up easily. Sometimes you must build it on purpose. It may look like creating a prayer text thread with two or three other women in business, scheduling monthly check-ins with a fellow entrepreneur, joining a Bible study where you can be real, asking someone to be your accountability partner (spiritually and professionally), or saying yes to safe spaces like Bible Babes where you don't have to pretend.

You don't need a crowd. You need a circle. One or two really rooted sisters can change everything.

Anchor Truth

Ecclesiastes 4:9–10 reminds you that two are better than one. When you fall, someone is there to help you up. Isolation is dangerous.

Galatians 6:2 teaches that carrying each other's burdens fulfills the law of Christ. You were never meant to carry everything alone.

Hebrews 10:24–25 calls you to encourage one another toward love and good deeds, and to not give up meeting together. Community is essential.

REFLECTION QUESTIONS

1. Have I been trying to carry too much alone? Why?

....

....

....

2. Who has God placed around me that I need to invite deeper into my journey?

....

....

....

3. Where do I need to stop performing and start allowing myself to be supported?

....

....

....

4. What would it look like to build intentionally in community, not just in isolation?

....

....

....

Time Wise Mastery Activity: Circle Check

List three women in your life who could be a spiritual or strategic covering for you in this season. Then ask, "Why did each woman come to mind for this season of my life?" Write how they strengthen, challenge, or inspire you and which qualities they possess that reflect where you want to grow personally. Prayerfully consider how consistently you are allowing these women to speak into your life.

Name	How She Supports or Inspires Me	Have I Let Her in Fully?	Next Step I'll Take to Deepen This Connection

Pro Tip for Busy Women in Business

Reach out to one woman this week who encourages you spiritually or professionally. Set up a coffee chat, a prayer call, or a simple check-in. Intentional community starts with one conversation.

DECLARATION

I was never meant to build alone. I release the lie
that I must carry everything by myself. I welcome
sisterhood, vulnerability, and shared strength. I will build
community on purpose and let others build into me. I
am covered, seen, supported, and surrounded by the
women God has placed in my life. Together, we rise.

PRAYER

Father,

As this week comes to a close, thank You for the insight and clarity You have given me. Help me apply what I have learned with confidence and peace. I choose to steward what is in my hands with faithfulness and trust You with what comes next.

In Jesus' name, Amen.

CLOSING ENCOURAGEMENT

You're not just a business builder. You're a pillar in the Kingdom. You don't need to be the strong one all the time. Even pillars need support. You don't need to show up fine just to be accepted. You are safe here. You are supported here. And you are stronger when you're surrounded. Keep building, but never build alone. We're in this together. Faithfully Flourishing isn't just a devotional workbook. It's a sisterhood of Kingdom-minded women rising together in purpose, rooted in faith, and flourishing for God's glory.

Stewarding What You've Built with Excellence & Order

This week marked a shift from striving to stewarding, from chaos to clarity, and from hustle to holy rhythm.

You have spent the past seven days learning what it truly means to steward well:

- Faithfulness rooted in God's pace,
  not the world's pressure
- Order created as an act of worship, not just productivity
- Boundaries set to protect what God has entrusted to you
- Rest received as a strategy, not just a reward
- Excellence chosen over perfection and performance
- Purpose aligned with peace instead of pressure
- Community embraced as your covering,
  not just your network

And through each day, one truth has become clearer: Your business is not just something you manage. It is something you steward for God's glory. You are not building alone. You are partnering with the God of order Himself.

You are not the same woman you were seven days ago. You've begun walking differently. You're more aware that slow growth is sacred growth, more grounded in the truth that order honors God, more steady in protecting your boundaries, more intentional about rest, more focused on excellence over perfection, more surrendered to God's purpose, more supported by community.

Your calling has started to shift from something that overwhelms you into something you're learning to steward with wisdom and peace.

Order is increasing. Chaos is decreasing. Boundaries are strengthening.

This week, you:

- Chose faithfulness over frantic growth,
  honoring small beginnings
- Created order as an act of worship, not just productivity
- Set boundaries to protect the blessing God has given you
- Received rest as a gift from God, not something to earn
- Chose excellence over perfection,
  releasing pressure to be flawless
- Aligned your business with purpose instead of pressure
- Embraced community as your covering,
  not just your network

You didn't just learn more about God's heart for stewardship. You began walking it out.

WHAT YOU'VE LEARNED THIS WEEK

Day 1 — Faithfulness Over Frantic Growth

Fast success is not always favored success. God values roots before fruit, integrity before visibility, and faithfulness over flashiness. Small beginnings are sacred.

Day 2 — Order Is a Form of Worship

God is not a God of disorder but of peace. When you bring order to your business, your time, and your space, you are inviting God to dwell more fully in it.

Day 3 — Boundaries Protect the Blessing

Boundaries are not selfish. They are sacred. Even Jesus had boundaries. When you protect your peace, you protect your purpose.

Day 4 — Rest Is a Strategy, Not a Reward

God rested not because He was tired, but because He was modeling the rhythm of life. Rest is how you recalibrate, return, and hear again.

Day 5 — Resist Worldly Perfection & Embrace Excellence

God doesn't anoint your perfection. He anoints your surrender. Excellence is about honoring God, not impressing others. Your work doesn't have to be flawless to be fruitful.

Day 6 — Purpose Over Pressure

God didn't call you to chase metrics. He called you to make a mark. Your yes is powerful, and that means it needs to be protected. Purpose brings peace.

Day 7 — Community Is Your Covering

You were never meant to build alone. Isolation is a strategy of the enemy. When you're surrounded by Spirit-led women, you become a force.

REFLECTION FOR THE WEEK

Take a moment today to pause and breathe. Look back over this week and ask yourself:

1. What truth from this week shifted the way I see myself as a woman in business?

....

....

....

2. What area of my business or leadership did I surrender back to God this week?

....

....

....

3. How did I experience God's presence in my work, schedule, or relationships?

....

....

....

4. Where did I feel stretched, and what do I believe God was growing in me through it?

....

....

....

5. What limiting belief, comparison, or fear did I release and lay at the feet of Jesus?

....

....

....

6. What idea, vision, or direction has God started to reveal for my next season?

....

....

....

7. Where am I invited to rest, recharge, and realign before moving forward?

....

....

....

Faithfulness doesn't grow in leaps. It grows in layers. And you have laid a beautiful, solid foundation.

Time Wise Mastery Review: Your Weekly Alignment

Take 20–30 minutes of quiet time to prayerfully answer these check-in questions:

What did I learn this week?

Where did I feel most aligned with God?

What truth am I still wrestling with?

What small win or fruit did I see?

What needs to shift in my mindset, schedule, or systems?

What is God asking me to surrender?

What is God asking me to step into?

Pro Tip for Busy Women in Business

Choose your favorite truth from this week and make it your "stewardship anchor" for the next seven days. Put it on your mirror, your phone, or your laptop. Let it steady your spirit every time you feel overwhelmed or pressured.

DECLARATION FOR THE WEEK AHEAD

I choose to be a faithful steward of what God has placed in my hands. I honor my business, my gifts, and my time. I trade overwhelm for wisdom. I lay down chaos and pick up order. I create space for rest and protect my boundaries with courage. I choose excellence over perfection, purpose over pressure, and community over isolation. I am not building for recognition. I am building for the Kingdom. And I will be found faithful.

PRAYER

Father God,

Thank You for the work You have done in my heart and mind this week. Thank You for showing me that stewardship is not about perfection, but about faithfulness. Help me carry forward the lessons of order, excellence, and intention as I continue building what You have entrusted to me.

I release control and choose trust. I commit my business, my time, and my decisions fully into Your hands. I move forward with clarity, peace, and confidence, knowing You are guiding every step.

In Jesus' name, Amen.

CLOSING ENCOURAGEMENT

The world will always push you toward more. But God is calling you back to stewardship. When you steward well, He multiplies it.

Stay rooted in this truth: Your greatest breakthrough may not come from starting something new, but from faithfully stewarding what you've already started.

Keep showing up. Keep creating order as worship. Keep protecting your peace. Keep choosing rest. Keep building with excellence.

You're not just managing a business. You're stewarding a calling. And Heaven sees every faithful choice.

LIVING COMPLETELY IN YOUR KINGDOM ASSIGNMENT

When I first started building my business, I was obsessed with results. Every week, I'd check the numbers, refresh the inbox, and measure my worth by what was happening around me. But God kept whispering something I didn't want to hear: "Just obey. Trust Me with the rest."

That felt too simple. Too risky. What if I obeyed and nothing happened?

But then I read John 15:5:

"I am the vine; you are the branches. If you remain in me and I in you, you will bear much fruit; apart from me you can do nothing."

And suddenly, I realized I'd been doing it backwards. God wasn't asking me to produce fruit. He was asking me to stay connected to Him through obedience, and He would handle the rest.

But obedience didn't always feel powerful. Sometimes it felt small. Quiet. Invisible.

There were seasons when I obeyed and saw no immediate results. I took steps of faith that no one applauded. I built with eternity in mind when the world celebrated what was trending. I kept walking when everything in me wanted to quit because the progress felt too slow.

But even in those hidden moments, God was at work. He was teaching me that my job is to obey, and His job is to produce the outcome. He was strengthening my faith muscle with every small yes. He was building spiritual stamina so I could finish faithfully, not just start strong.

Every act of obedience, even the ones that felt insignificant, was actually sacred ground. Every moment I chose courage over comfort mattered more than I realized.

If you're reading this and wondering if your obedience counts when you can't see the fruit yet, know this: it does. God sees every faithful step. Your obedience is never wasted. The harvest is coming because you kept planting in faith.

You were created to walk in faith. You were chosen to build for eternity. As you begin this week, remember: Your obedience, your perseverance, and your courage are sacred acts of worship. You are partnering with God Himself to build something that echoes in eternity.

Step forward with boldness, and celebrate the movement that isn't visible on the outside but matters deeply in the Kingdom of God.

This week builds the foundation for walking in faithful obedience:

- In your obedience when you trust that
  faithfulness leads to overflow
- In your faith when you strengthen your spiritual
  muscle through action, not just belief
- In your vision when you build with eternity
  in mind, not external validation
- In your perseverance when you keep walking
  even when progress feels invisible
- In your courage when you choose boldness
  over the comfort of playing it safe
- In your surrender when you release outcomes
  and trust God's perfect process
- In your endurance when you commit to
  finishing faithfully, not just starting strong

This week moves you from hesitation to holy action, builds faith through obedience, and grounds you in the truth that obedience is your job while outcomes belong to God. You'll learn to choose courage over comfort and perseverance over pressure, trusting that fruit follows faithfulness.

By the end of Week 3, you will feel:

- More confident that obedience leads to overflow, even when you can't see it yet
- More aware that faith grows through movement, not just meditation
- More certain that building for eternity matters more than building for validation
- More equipped to persevere through slow seasons without doubting your calling
- More courageous in choosing God's call over cultural comfort
- More peaceful in surrendering outcomes to God's perfect timing
- More committed to finishing faithfully what God started in you

This week is about becoming a woman who obeys before she understands. It is about becoming faithful in the unseen seasons. It is about becoming steady in the truth that fruitfulness flows from faithfulness, not from forcing results.

Your calling to flourish is not dependent on immediate outcomes, public approval, or perfect circumstances. You are partnering with God Himself, and He is producing eternal fruit through your faithful yes.

This is your week to rise grounded, anchored, and confident in the calling God has placed on your life.

You've spent the last two weeks creating space for God to refine your heart, your business, and your vision. You've chosen alignment over hustle, faith over fear, and purpose over pressure.

Now, it's time to move forward, not with striving, but with obedient action rooted in surrender.

When Jesus said, "Remain in Me," He wasn't offering a formula for success. He was giving us a rhythm for fruitfulness. The more we stay connected to Him through obedience, the more our lives produce what truly matters: peace, purpose, endurance, and Kingdom impact.

You weren't called to control every outcome. You weren't called to impress the world. You were called to obey, to persevere, and to trust that faithful action produces eternal fruit.

That's the difference between worldly ambition and faithful flourishing.

This devotional journey may be wrapping up, but your walk of obedience is just beginning. Your yes is not about building a business that trends. It's about building a life that testifies.

So, as you step into what's next, remember: you don't have to feel ready. You don't have to see the full picture. You just have to walk with the One who called you.

Let Him lead. Let Him grow the fruit. Let Him finish what He started in you. He's not looking for perfection. He's looking for your faithful yes.

Keep showing up. Keep planting in faith. Keep walking forward, not for the approval of others, but for His glory.

This final week isn't a conclusion. It's a commissioning.

DAILY CHALLENGE

As you prepare for Week 3, ask the Holy Spirit to give you a word to carry as a banner.

Circle one or write your own:

Obedience | Boldness | Faith | Courage | Perseverance | Surrender | Overflow | Rooted | Focus | Endurance

Write it big. Write it proudly. Write it where you'll see it daily.

You're not just building a business. You're building a life that advances the Kingdom of Heaven.

OBEDIENCE OVER OUTCOME

Wisdom from the Word

"But Samuel replied: 'Does the LORD delight in burnt offerings and sacrifices as much as in obeying the LORD? To obey is better than sacrifice, and to heed is better than the fat of rams.'"
  1 Samuel 15:22

"When he had finished speaking, he said to Simon, 'Put out into deep water, and let down the nets for a catch.' Simon answered, 'Master, we've worked hard all night and haven't caught anything. But because you say so, I will let down the nets.' When they had done so, they caught such a large number of fish that their nets began to break."
  Luke 5:4–6

"Commit to the LORD whatever you do, and he will establish your plans."
  Proverbs 16:3

ANCHORED IN THE LORD: Flourishing Foundations & Grounded Growth

Obedience sounds spiritual until it costs you something. Until you have to launch without likes, speak when your voice shakes, serve without being seen, give when you feel empty, stay when you want to run, or go when you're afraid to move.

Obedience is holy, yes, but also humbling. Because it asks you to release control, to show up without a guarantee, and to plant seeds you may never see bloom. And yet, this is the path God blesses.

In Luke 5, Peter had every reason to ignore Jesus' instruction. He was a professional fisherman. He knew the water, the timing, the rhythm. He had already toiled all night and come up empty. But when Jesus said, "Put out into the deep water," Peter didn't argue. He didn't calculate the odds. He said, "Because You say so."

And that moment of obedience turned an empty net into a supernatural overflow.

Let that sink in: the same place where Peter failed in his own strength became the place of breakthrough in God's timing. And the same will be true for you.

You may have posted the offer already, tried the ad, had the hard conversation, or launched the thing, and watched no one sign up. But what if the shift doesn't come because of what changes around you? What if it comes because of what changes in you? God's miracles often follow a move of obedience.

We often want proof before the launch, strategy before the surrender, and certainty before the step. But God often says, "Trust Me. Take the step. I'll show you the rest later."

Obedience is what unlocks momentum in the Kingdom. It's not just a good idea. It's a divine alignment.

We resist obedience because we've been trained to measure value by results, not by response to God. We think:

- "What if I mess up the timing?"
- "What if it flops?"
- "What if people don't respond?"
- "What if I misunderstood God?"

But God is not fragile. He's not evaluating you like a professor grading your business plan. He's looking for a heart that trusts Him more than the world's metrics.

And the beautiful thing is that even when you're unsure, even when your step is shaky, God still calls it faith. He blesses the woman who moves not because she feels ready, but because she knows the One who called her is faithful.

So, what's your next step? Not the perfect one. Not the flashy one. Not the one that guarantees results. Just the faithful one. The one that says, "God, this isn't about what I'll get from it. It's about honoring You through it."

That's obedience. And obedience is never wasted.

Anchor Truth

1 Samuel 15:22 reminds you that obedience is better than sacrifice. God values a heart that follows His voice over religious performance.

Luke 5:4–6 shows that obedience, even when it doesn't make sense, can lead to breakthrough. Peter obeyed, and his nets filled.

Proverbs 16:3 anchors you in surrender. When you yield your pace to His direction, God faithfully establishes your steps.

REFLECTION QUESTIONS

1. What step has God been nudging me to take that I've been delaying out of fear of the outcome?

....

....

....

2. Where have I made obedience harder than it needs to be?

....

....

....

3. What does success look like from Heaven's perspective, not just mine?

....

....

....

4. What would it feel like to obey, even if the results are unseen?

....

....

....

Time Wise Mastery Activity: The Obedience Tracker

Choose one thing God has asked you to do this month, even if it's small. Track your obedience, not the result.

What God Prompted Me to Do	I Took the Step (Yes/No)	What Happened in My Heart When I Did/Didn't

Pro Tip for Busy Women in Business

Write down one step of obedience God has been prompting you to take. Set a date to do it, and tell one trusted friend for accountability. Obedience grows when you take it out of your head and into action.

DECLARATION

I release the pressure to produce outcomes. I trust that God honors my obedience more than perfection. I say yes to what He's asking of me today. I will walk in faith, not fear. I will build from a place of trust, not control. My obedience is my offering, and I trust God with the rest.

PRAYER

Father God,

Thank You for leading me into what is next. Even when the path feels uncertain, I trust that You are guiding my steps. Help me walk forward with courage and obedience, confident that You go before me. I place my faith in You as I move ahead.

In Jesus' name, Amen.

CLOSING ENCOURAGEMENT

Your obedience may feel small to you, but it echoes in Heaven. You're not responsible for what happens after the yes. You're only responsible for the yes itself. Let this bring you peace today: God doesn't need you to know how it will work. He just asks you to believe that He will do immeasurably more than you could ask or imagine.

FAITH IS A MUSCLE

Wisdom from the Word

"Now faith is confidence in what we hope for and assurance about what we do not see."
        Hebrews 11:1

"Consequently, faith comes from hearing the message, and the message is heard through the word about Christ."
        Romans 10:17

"He replied, 'Because you have so little faith. Truly I tell you, if you have faith as small as a mustard seed, you can say to this mountain, "Move from here to there," and it will move. Nothing will be impossible for you.'"
        Matthew 17:20

ANCHORED IN THE LORD: Flourishing Foundations & Grounded Growth

Some days you wake up filled with fire. You're ready to run, launch, speak, and believe. You feel the presence of God so close you could almost touch it. And on those days, faith feels easy, natural, alive.

But then there are the other days when you feel stuck in the fog, when you question everything you're building, when prayers feel quiet, when results feel distant, when you wake up and the only words you can muster are, "God, help."

That doesn't make you weak. That doesn't make you unqualified. That doesn't mean you're failing. That makes you human. And more importantly, it makes you a candidate for growth.

We often imagine faith as a feeling: that surge of motivation after a good sermon, that bold moment in prayer when it all feels clear, that rush of confidence when something just clicks. But that's not the full story because faith isn't a personality trait. It's not reserved for the brave, the bubbly, the bold, or the ones who never waver.

Faith is a muscle. And just like your body, it only gets stronger when it's used. Muscles grow through resistance, through stretching, through pressure, through motion. And so does your faith.

When Jesus talked about mustard seed faith, He wasn't dismissing small faith. He was dignifying it. He was saying: You don't have to move the mountain. Just plant the seed. I'll handle the rest. You don't need to be confident. You just need to be convinced that He's good. You don't need a full map. Just enough light for the next step. You don't need to have it all together. Just enough trust to obey anyway.

Your yes, your whisper, your first step—they're enough because when placed in the hands of a faithful God, even the smallest seed can move the greatest mountain.

We love the idea of growing in faith. But growth doesn't happen in stillness. It happens in the stretch. You can fill journals with vision, listen to podcast after podcast, and read every devotional and verse, but your faith doesn't mature in theory. It matures in movement.

It grows when you say yes before you feel ready, speak when your voice trembles, obey when the instructions don't make sense, create before you feel qualified, and keep showing up, even after disappointment. Because every step you take, no matter how small, is a rep in the gym of spiritual growth.

Faith is not about the size of your belief. It's about the direction of your trust.

The enemy will whisper:

- "You'll fail if you try."
- "You're not ready."
- "You missed your moment."
- "Who do you think you are to step out like that?"

But God whispers louder:

- "You're mine."
- "I'll go before you."
- "Just start. I'll finish it."
- "You don't have to be perfect. You just have to be present."

Fear wants to freeze you. But faith wants to form you. Fear says, "Sit this one out." Faith says, "Step in. God's got you."

So today, let this be your gentle reminder: you don't need big, flashy faith to make a move. You just need mustard seed faith and a willingness to plant it. Because God isn't looking for your polish. He's looking for your participation. And every time you trust Him, even a little more than yesterday, you are building spiritual muscle that will sustain you through every season to come.

Anchor Truth

Hebrews 11:1 reminds you that faith is confidence in what you hope for and assurance about what you don't yet see. You don't need to see everything to trust Him.

Romans 10:17 teaches that faith comes from hearing the message about Christ. Keep filling your mind with His Word, and your faith will grow.

Matthew 17:20 shows that even the smallest faith can move mountains. You don't need perfect faith. You just need to take the next step.

REFLECTION QUESTIONS

1. What's one area of my life or business where I've been waiting to feel more confident before taking a step?

....

....

....

2. What's a small act of obedience I can take today to stretch my faith muscle?

....

....

....

3. What past moment in my life proves that when I trusted God, He showed up for me?

....

....

....

Time Wise Mastery Activity: Faith Reps Tracker

Using the following examples, carve out a space in your journal or calendar to track your daily acts of faith, no matter how small. Each one is a rep, and each rep matters.

Faith Action I Took	How I Felt Before	How I Felt After	What I Learned About God
Sent the client the pitch email	Nervous	Relieved & hopeful	He honors movement.
Prayed aloud for my business for 10 mins	Disconnected	Peaceful & focused	He meets me when I show up.
Shared my story publicly for the first time	Vulnerable	Empowered	God uses my story more than I realized.

Pro Tip for Busy Women in Business

Start a "Faith Wins" journal where you record every time you stepped out in faith and God showed up. When doubt creeps in, review it to remind yourself that God has always been faithful.

DECLARATION

My faith is growing stronger every day. I don't need to have it all figured out to walk forward. I trust God with the next step, even if it feels small. My faith may start as a seed, but it carries the power of Heaven. I am not waiting for confidence. I am walking in conviction.

PRAYER

Lord,

When fear or doubt tries to slow me down, remind me of Your promises. Help me release hesitation and step forward with confidence rooted in You. I trust that You will equip me for everything You are calling me to do.

In Jesus' name, Amen.

CLOSING ENCOURAGEMENT

Every small act of faith is spiritual strength training. You don't have to bench press mountains today. You only have to move the mustard seed. And over time, that quiet consistency will become a loud testimony. So, take your step today, even if it's small. God will meet you there.

BUILD WITH THE END IN MIND

Wisdom from the Word

"Do not store up for yourselves treasures on earth, where moths and vermin destroy, and where thieves break in and steal. But store up for yourselves treasures in heaven, where moths and vermin do not destroy, and where thieves do not break in and steal. For where your treasure is, there your heart will be also."
>   Matthew 6:19–21

"I have fought the good fight, I have finished the race, I have kept the faith."
>   2 Timothy 4:7

"Set your minds on things above, not on earthly things."
>   Colossians 3:2

ANCHORED IN THE LORD: Flourishing Foundations & Grounded Growth

You didn't start your business just to pay the bills. Yes, income matters. You have goals, responsibilities, and dreams for your family. But deep down, you know that God stirred something more in you.

You're building something bigger, something that outlives trends and outlasts the noise, something that changes lives (not just shopping carts), and something that reflects the heart of God, even when no one clicks, buys, or says thank you. Your hands may be building a brand, a product, or a platform, but your heart is building legacy.

You start with passion and purpose. You dream with God, write the vision, pray over the plan. But then the inbox piles up. The numbers don't match your expectations. The algorithm shifts. The pressure to keep up creeps in.

You start comparing yourself to others who seem further ahead. You feel guilty if you rest. You feel behind if you're not constantly producing. You start questioning your pace, your purpose, even your calling. And suddenly, without meaning to, you're no longer building from overflow. You're building from exhaustion. You're just crossing things off a list, but your soul feels disconnected from your why.

In Matthew 6:19-21, Jesus gently reminds us: "Do not store up for yourselves treasures on earth, but store up treasures in heaven. For where your treasure is, there your heart will be also."

Take a holy pause to ask: Am I building something that will matter in eternity?

It may not feel like it when you're editing emails, packaging orders, or scheduling posts, but every Kingdom-centered action, no matter how small, is sacred: every encouraging word to a client, every behind-the-scenes prayer before a meeting, every moment you choose honesty over hype, every time you serve with joy (even when you're tired), every boundary you hold to protect your peace, and every offering you release in faith.

None of it is wasted. It's not just business. It's ministry in motion, your obedience woven into your creativity, your surrender shaping your strategy. That's what God sees. That's what Heaven multiplies (not the algorithm, not the applause, not even the accolades). What you build in faith lasts forever.

Can you imagine Paul, nearing the end of his life, saying, "I went viral," "I sold out," or "I scaled to seven figures"? Of course not! Instead, he said, "I have fought the good fight. I have finished the race. I have kept the faith."

That's the goal: to stay faithful to the assignment God gave you, even when it looks different than hers; to walk at Heaven's pace, not hustle culture's; and to build with love, with purpose, with eternity in mind.

So today, before you create another offer or refresh your stats, pause and ask: "Am I building something that reflects the heart of the King, or am I chasing something that simply looks impressive on the surface?" Because the Kingdom isn't impressed by your performance. It's moved by your faithfulness.

Come back to the foundation. Not your five-year plan, not your Pinterest mood board, and not your launch calendar. Come back to the moment God called you, the burden He gave you to carry, the people He uniquely positioned you to serve, and the story you've been entrusted to live and tell.

This is holy ground. And your business is not separate from your spiritual life. It's an extension of it.

Eternal building looks like prioritizing people over platforms, loving your clients (not just landing them), holding room for rest (not just revenue), staying in integrity (even when it's costly), partnering with the Holy Spirit in every decision, choosing peace over pressure, and finishing with faithfulness.

Anchor Truth

Matthew 6:19–21 reminds you to store up treasures in Heaven, not on earth. Where your treasure is, there your heart will be also.

2 Timothy 4:7 shows that finishing faithfully matters more than finishing first. Paul's legacy was his faithfulness to the calling.

Colossians 3:2 teaches you to set your mind on things above, not on earthly things. Keep your focus on what matters eternally.

REFLECTION QUESTIONS

1. Have I been building more for visibility or for legacy?

....

....

....

2. What part of my business do I want to be remembered for most?

....

....

....

3. What does faithful finishing look like in my current season?

....

....

....

4. What eternal fruit do I pray will come from the seeds I'm planting right now?

....

....

....

Time Wise Mastery Activity: Vision Alignment Map

Let's realign your business actions with your eternal why. Here are some examples to get you started:

What I'm Building	The Fruit I Pray It Bears	The Eternal Impact I Hope It Has
Boutique with faith-based apparel	Confidence & identity rooted in Christ	That women would feel seen, bold, and beautiful in truth
Real estate services	Trust, comfort, peace for families	That homes would be filled with God's presence & provision
Aesthetics	Restoration, confidence, healing	That every woman would feel seen, nurtured, and reminded she is fearfully and wonderfully made, beautiful inside and out

Pro Tip for Busy Women in Business

Write your eternal "why" on a sticky note and place it where you work. Before making business decisions, check them against your why by asking yourself, "Does this align with the legacy I'm building?"

DECLARATION

I build with eternity in mind. I release the pressure to chase what fades, and I choose to steward what lasts. I am not working for praise. I am working for impact. I commit my business, my plans, and my hands to the Lord. I will finish this race faithfully, knowing my reward is found in Him.

PRAYER

God,

Thank You for reminding me that obedience often requires action before understanding. Help me trust You even when I cannot see the full picture. Strengthen my faith as I take the next right step, knowing You are faithful to lead me.

In Jesus' name, Amen.

CLOSING ENCOURAGEMENT

What you are building matters. Not just for this quarter, this client, or this campaign, but for generations to come. You are planting seeds you may never fully see bloom, but Heaven sees. Heaven records. And Heaven multiplies. So stay the course. Stay faithful. This is how we build a legacy of flourishing faithfully.

When You Feel Stuck, Keep Walking

Wisdom from the Word

"The LORD makes firm the steps of the one who delights in him; though he may stumble, he will not fall, for the LORD upholds him with his hand."
   Psalm 37:23–24

"Whether you turn to the right or to the left, your ears will hear a voice behind you, saying, 'This is the way; walk in it.'"
   Isaiah 30:21

"Let us not become weary in doing good, for at the proper time we will reap a harvest if we do not give up."
   Galatians 6:9

ANCHORED IN THE LORD: Flourishing Foundations & Grounded Growth

Some days you just feel stuck. Not lazy, not unmotivated, and not rebellious. Just stuck.

You might feel like your soul is trying to move, but the ground feels heavy. Your heart remembers the vision, but your body feels too tired to chase it. The fire you once had has simmered into embers, and now you're wondering if there's anything left to fan back into flame.

Maybe you've hit a dry spell in your business and you're starting to question your ability. Maybe the clarity you once had is clouded by uncertainty. Maybe you're running on empty, juggling your clients, your calendar, your kids, your calling, and you wonder if there's anything left in you to pour out.

And in that still, tired space, the questions creep in:

- "Did I miss something?"
- "Was I ever really called to this?"
- "Did I take a wrong turn?"
- "Is God still with me?"

You didn't miss something. You really are called. Every turn is in God's hands. He is always with you.

God doesn't leave you when it feels slow. He leads you, even in the silence. He's not measuring your progress by what others can see. He's not disappointed in your pace. And He's not waiting for you to get it all together before He moves again. Sometimes the stillness isn't punishment. It's preparation.

He's doing deep work in the unseen places, strengthening your roots so your fruit can last, protecting you from rushing into things that look good but aren't God, and refining your faith so your next yes is anchored in obedience, not outcome.

There is a sacred kind of slowness where God teaches you how to walk with Him again. Not sprint. Not strive. Just walk: one step, one whisper, one breath, one act of trust.

It's in these slower seasons where He breaks off the need to be seen and replaces it with a desire to be steady. He invites you to cling to His voice instead of your visibility. He teaches you that success is not speed but surrender. He shows you that sometimes the most obedient thing you can do is stay rooted when everything in you wants to run.

The enemy will try to paralyze you in seasons like this. He'll say,

- "You're not doing enough."
- "You missed your moment."

- "Everyone else is ahead of you."
- "You should just quit."

But the Spirit of God says, "Daughter, just take the next step. I've got the map. I see the future. And I'm still writing your story."

Even if that step is as simple as praying when you feel dry, opening your journal again, sending one brave email, honoring your Sabbath, sitting with a mentor, asking for help, or starting the project (even if no one notices).

That's still movement. That's still faith. That's still Kingdom ground being claimed in your name. Because even when it feels like nothing is changing, you are becoming.

You are growing deeper, stronger, more aligned with God's plan. And God always honors faithfulness, even when it's quiet.

He's not done. He hasn't forgotten the promise. And He's not waiting for you to feel perfect before He partners with your next step.

You may not be where you want to be. But you're not where you were. And that is movement. You are becoming more patient, more surrendered, more secure in your identity, more rooted in your values, and more dependent on His voice.

This isn't a delay. It's divine development. So keep going, even if your pace is slower than you'd like, even if you have more questions than answers, and even if it feels like no one sees what you're pushing through. Your Father in Heaven sees. Your steps are sacred. And your obedience is unlocking something deeper than momentum. It's unlocking maturity.

So don't give up now. You are walking toward something far greater than a business milestone. You're walking into a life that echoes in eternity.

Anchor Truth

Psalm 37:23–24 reminds you that the Lord makes firm the steps of the one who delights in Him. Even when you stumble, you will not fall. He upholds you.

Isaiah 30:21 teaches that God's voice will guide you. Whether you turn to the right or left, He will say, "This is the way; walk in it."

Galatians 6:9 encourages you not to become weary in doing good. At the proper time, you will reap a harvest if you don't give up.

REFLECTION QUESTIONS

1. Where in my business or calling have I felt stuck or unclear?

....

....

....

2. What is one faithful step I can take today to move forward, even if it's small?

....

....

....

3. How can I remind myself that slow seasons can still be sacred?

....

....

....

4. What truth about God's character do I need to cling to while I wait?

....

....

....

Time Wise Mastery Activity:
The Still Moving List

Make a list of faithful steps you've taken recently, even if the results haven't shown up yet. Here are some examples:

Step I Took	Why It Mattered
Texted a friend a prayer and words of encouragement	Reminded her she's not walking alone
Sent a proposal even though I was nervous	Chose faith over fear
Took a day of rest when I felt overwhelmed	Honored God with my boundaries
Prayed before my business meeting	Invited the Holy Spirit into my work

Pro Tip for Busy Women in Business

Keep a "faithful steps" journal. Each week, write down one small act of obedience you took, even if no results followed. Over time, you'll see that God honors every step of faith.

DECLARATION

Even when I feel stuck, I will keep walking. God is with me in the slow seasons and the silent ones. My steps are ordered, my heart is secure, and my future is in His hands. I will not be moved by what I don't see. I will be anchored in who He is.

PRAYER

Father,

Teach me to walk with patience and confidence, not rushing ahead or holding back in fear. Help me stay aligned with Your timing and remain attentive to Your guidance. I desire to move forward with peace and trust in You.

In Jesus' name, Amen.

CLOSING ENCOURAGEMENT

Your progress doesn't have to be loud to be holy. If you're still praying, still showing up, still leaning in, you're moving. Don't despise the season where it looks like nothing is happening. Often, that's when everything is being prepared. He's not just making a way. He's making you ready. So take the step. Even if you're unsure. Even if you're tired. He'll meet you in the movement.

COURAGE OVER COMFORT

Wisdom from the Word

"Have I not commanded you? Be strong and courageous. Do not be afraid; do not be discouraged, for the LORD your God will be with you wherever you go."
> Joshua 1:9

"But he said to me, 'My grace is sufficient for you, for my power is made perfect in weakness.' Therefore I will boast all the more gladly about my weaknesses, so that Christ's power may rest on me."
> 2 Corinthians 12:9

"The wicked flee though no one pursues, but the righteous are as bold as a lion."
> Proverbs 28:1

ANCHORED IN THE LORD: Flourishing Foundations & Grounded Growth

Choosing courage over comfort in this day and age feels radical. The world tells you to build your brand, stay polished, keep it safe, and only share what's guaranteed to get engagement or validation.

But Faithfully Flourishing was never about playing it safe. It's about building something eternal in a culture that values what's immediate, obeying God when no one's clapping, and continuing to show up, even when results feel slow.

The world rewards what's loud, shiny, and viral. But God rewards what's obedient, humble, and bold in spirit. And real courage, the kind that moves mountains, often looks nothing like the culture's definition of success.

You may feel pressure to stay small (so you don't make others uncomfortable), wait until it's perfect (so you don't get criticized), blend in (so you're not misunderstood), or say what's popular (instead of what's powerful).

But you weren't called to blend. You were called to burn. You were created to carry fire, not fear. And fire doesn't hide. It illuminates.

In today's marketplace, comfort often masquerades as wisdom. We convince ourselves it's wise to delay, stay quiet, or wait until we have it all figured out. But often, that's just fear in disguise.

We live in a time when everyone is building something: a platform, a following, a funnel, a name. But you? You're building for the Kingdom. And Kingdom builders must live differently. We don't move based on fear, metrics, or optics. We move when God says move, even if we're shaking. Because the women who change the world are not the ones who played it safe. They are the ones who heard God's voice, felt the fear, and did it anyway.

So today, if you feel small, good. That means there's room for God to be big. And if you feel scared, perfect. Because bravery isn't the absence of fear. It's moving in the face of it. God doesn't need your comfort. He's after your courage.

To faithfully flourish in this generation means you're willing to say yes when others hesitate, speak truth when others remain silent, launch the thing when no one else understands it, choose integrity even when it costs, and trust God's timeline over pressure to perform.

Your boldness might not trend. Your obedience might not go viral. But in God's eyes, you're doing Kingdom work. And His is the only record that matters. Every courageous yes matters more than you know.

So even when your knees shake, take the step. Even when your voice trembles, speak. Even when your plan isn't perfect, go anyway. You are a woman of valor, a daughter of the King, and a builder of things that last.

So today, let courage rise because the comfort zone is too small for the calling on your life.

Anchor Truth

Joshua 1:9 reminds you that God commands you to be strong and courageous. He will be with you wherever you go. You don't walk alone.

2 Corinthians 12:9 teaches that God's grace is sufficient and His power is made perfect in weakness. You don't need to be strong on your own.

Proverbs 28:1 shows that the righteous are as bold as a lion. When you walk with God, courage rises within you.

REFLECTION QUESTIONS

1. Where in my life or business am I choosing comfort over courage?

....

....

....

2. What is one bold move God may be prompting me to take, even if it feels risky?

....

....

....

3. What fear have I been allowing to shape my decisions?

....

....

....

4. How would my business look if I led more courageously and less comfortably?

....

....

....

Time Wise Mastery Activity: Courage Over Comfort Audit

Use the table below to evaluate where you're staying safe, and where you're being invited to be bold. I've added some common examples for Christian women in business to get you started.

Area of My Life or Business	Comfort Zone Behavior	Courage-Driven Action I Will Take
Setting boundaries with clients	Saying yes to everything to please others	Honor my limits and protect what God has entrusted to me
Asking for help or feedback	Staying silent to appear capable	Reach out and let others support me
Pricing my services	Undervaluing out of fear of rejection	Charge fairly, trusting God to send the right people

Pro Tip for Busy Women in Business

Identify one area where fear is holding you back. Write down the courageous action you know you should take, set a deadline, and ask one trusted friend to hold you accountable.

DECLARATION

I choose courage over comfort. I will not let fear decide
for me. I was not created to play small. I was called to
carry Kingdom light. The Holy Spirit is my confidence,
my comfort, and my guide. I will speak, move, and
lead boldly because the Lord goes before me.

PRAYER

Lord,

Thank You for walking with me through uncertainty and growth. When challenges arise, help me remain grounded in truth and anchored in faith. I trust that You are using every step to shape and strengthen me.

In Jesus' name, Amen.

CLOSING ENCOURAGEMENT

You don't have to be fearless to be faithful. You just need to take the step. And remember, courage doesn't mean the absence of fear. It means trusting God's presence in the middle of it. So, lift your head, raise your voice, and take the leap. Bold obedience is where breakthrough begins.

SURRENDER THE OUTCOME

Wisdom from the Word

"Trust in the LORD with all your heart and lean not on your own understanding; in all your ways submit to him, and he will make your paths straight."
　　　Proverbs 3:5–6

"I planted the seed, Apollos watered it, but God has been making it grow. So neither the one who plants nor the one who waters is anything, but only God, who makes things grow."
　　　1 Corinthians 3:6–7

"Commit your way to the LORD; trust in him and he will do this."
　　　Psalm 37:5

ANCHORED IN THE LORD: Flourishing Foundations & Grounded Growth

There comes a moment in every Kingdom builder's journey when you realize something sacred and sobering: you can control the seed, choose the soil, steward the strategy, water the work, and show up with faith. You can create the content, send the email, make the pitch, and pray over the outcome. But you still cannot control the harvest.

You can't control who signs the contract, who shows up to your event, who follows through, who shares your post, who sees the value in what you offer, or how quickly it grows.

And as frustrating as that can feel, it's also one of the most freeing truths you can embrace. Because Faithfully Flourishing isn't about chasing results. It's about releasing the pressure to be the source of them.

We live in a world that teaches us to idolize results: numbers, followers, profits, metrics, engagement, growth charts, algorithms. But God doesn't count what the world counts. He counts faithfulness.

In 1 Corinthians 3:6, Paul's words are both convicting and comforting: "I planted, Apollos watered, but God made it grow."

Do you hear the invitation in that? You're not the source, the miracle worker, or the growth generator. What you are is the vessel. You plant, water, and do your part in excellence, prayer, and stewardship. And then, you surrender.

That means you can stop striving to make things happen in your own strength, stop obsessing over whether enough people saw it, liked it, or bought it, and breathe again, knowing that your obedience was not wasted. Because even when the results don't reflect what you hoped, God is still at work beneath the surface.

Surrender isn't passive. It's powerful. Surrender isn't quitting or giving up because it's hard. It's giving it back to the One who owns it all anyway.

It's saying, "God, I've done my part. I've built in faith. Now I lay this in Your hands. You know what I need. You know who it's for. You know how and when it will bear fruit. I will not carry pressure You never asked me to hold."

God never wastes a surrendered offering. Not a single post, product, service, prayer, or plan offered with pure intention and obedience goes unseen by Him.

Even when you think it flopped, even when the response was small, even when no one applauded or celebrated you, God saw.

And He is working in ways you cannot yet see: in the hearts of clients, in the timing of opportunities, in the protection of your energy, and in the unseen doors that are opening while you're resting.

Some fruit grows in silence. Some answers are hidden in pruning. And sometimes, delay is His mercy, not His absence.

Here's what surrender really looks like in business: showing up in obedience (not outcome obsession), honoring God with excellence (not perfectionism), and releasing control and receiving peace.

You can still plan, promote, and pursue. But do it with open hands. Because clenched fists might feel strong, but they can't receive new grace.

If you want to Faithfully Flourish, you must trust that God's timing is better than your timeline, God's outcome is greater than your vision board, and God's covering is stronger than your control.

You don't flourish by pushing harder. You flourish by trusting deeper, because when your hands are open, your heart is light. A light heart is fertile ground for God's glory to grow.

So today, don't just surrender the outcome. Surrender the pressure, the performance, and the need to prove. And rest in this truth: God is the Gardener. You are the vessel. And He never forgets the seed you planted in faith.

Anchor Truth

Proverbs 3:5–6 reminds you to trust in the Lord with all your heart, not your own understanding. When you submit to Him, He will make your paths straight.

1 Corinthians 3:6–7 teaches that you plant and water, but God makes things grow. You're not the source. He is.

Psalm 37:5 invites you to commit your way to the Lord and trust in Him. He will do what needs to be done.

REFLECTION QUESTIONS

1. What outcome have I been gripping tightly out of fear or pressure?

....

....

....

2. Where have I attached my worth to a specific result or performance?

....

....

....

3. What would it look like for me to give that outcome back to God in trust?

....

....

....

4. How might surrender set me free to flourish?

....

....

....

Time Wise Mastery Activity: Your Surrender List

Write down the outcomes, results, or pressures you've been holding onto. Then, prayerfully surrender each one to God. To get your wheels turning, here's some inspiration:

What I've Been Holding Onto	My Prayer of Release
The need to hit a specific income goal	"Lord, I trust You to provide what I need in Your way and timing."
How many people bought something	"I release the pressure to perform and receive Your peace instead."
Worry about being misunderstood	"I choose obedience over approval. You are my defender."
The pace of growth in my business	"Even slow progress is sacred. You are not in a rush, and neither am I."

Pro Tip for Busy Women in Business

At the end of each day this week, write down one thing you did in obedience and one outcome you're surrendering to God. Practice releasing control while celebrating faithfulness.

DECLARATION

I surrender the outcome. I choose obedience over outcome, faith over fear, peace over pressure. I trust that what God started, He will finish in His way, in His time, for His glory. I am faithfully flourishing, and He is faithfully working.

PRAYER

God,

I release the need to have everything figured out. Help me remain open, obedient, and willing as You lead me forward. I choose faith over fear and trust You with both the process and the outcome.

In Jesus' name, Amen.

CLOSING ENCOURAGEMENT

You are not behind, forgotten, or failing. You are planting in faith. You are trusting in truth. You are surrendering the pressure to the One who holds it all. So, let go of the outcome today, and watch what God can do when your hands are open and your heart is aligned. The harvest will come because the faith was real.

Finish Faithfully

Wisdom from the Word

"… Forgetting what is behind and straining toward what is ahead, I press on toward the goal to win the prize for which God has called me heavenward in Christ Jesus."
>   Philippians 3:13–14

"The end of a matter is better than its beginning, and patience is better than pride."
>   Ecclesiastes 7:8

"Therefore, since we are surrounded by such a great cloud of witnesses, let us throw off everything that hinders and the sin that so easily entangles. And let us run with perseverance the race marked out for us, fixing our eyes on Jesus, the pioneer and perfecter of faith. For the joy set before him he endured the cross, scorning its shame, and sat down at the right hand of the throne of God."
>   Hebrews 12:1–2

ANCHORED IN THE LORD: Flourishing Foundations & Grounded Growth

If there's one thing our culture celebrates, it's starting: the bold announcement, the big launch, the polished branding, the first sale, the wave of excitement that comes with doing something new.

We glorify beginnings. We cheer when the website goes live, when the LLC is formed, when the dream is declared.

While those are beautiful moments worth honoring, they're not the full story. In the Kingdom of God, starting is important, but finishing is where the fruit lives.

Satan doesn't get nervous when you make a vision board. He doesn't panic when you brainstorm, journal, or even plan in prayer. But the moment you stay committed, the moment you keep showing up without recognition, the moment you keep saying yes when it's not exciting anymore, that's when he trembles. Because you're now building in faith.

So, what does he do? He targets the middle. He sends discouragement when it feels like no one is noticing. He whispers lies like, "This isn't working," or "You're wasting your time." He stirs up comparison to make you question your pace and your value. He tempts you to shift your focus from faithfulness to visibility. Because if he can't stop your start, he'll try to sabotage your stamina.

But here's what the enemy always underestimates: the power of a woman who knows she's been sent.

Faithfully Flourishing means you stay. Not because it's easy. Not because it's glamorous. But because God called you, and you've learned to trust His process more than your feelings.

You may not have a perfect track record. You may have taken breaks, cried through deadlines, or pivoted a dozen times. But you stayed. You stayed planted when the soil felt dry. You stayed faithful when others walked away. You stayed committed to integrity when shortcuts looked tempting. You stayed close to Jesus, even when the fog made the finish line hard to see.

That's what Faithfully Flourishing looks like in real life. It's not a highlight reel. It's a quiet, consistent yes to God, over and over again.

Paul didn't say, "I had a great start." He said: "I have fought the good fight, I have finished the race, I have kept the faith."

Those words carry the weight of a life lived with grit, grace, and grit again; a life that didn't quit when the crowd thinned out, didn't compromise when the pressure increased, and knew obedience was greater than outcome.

That's your calling, too. Not to burn out in the hustle, not to fizzle out when you get tired, and not to drop the baton because you're unsure who's watching. But to finish with your faith intact.

To look back and say, "I didn't always feel strong, but I stayed. I didn't always feel inspired, but I obeyed. I didn't always have answers, but I kept my eyes on Jesus." That's not just winning. That's flourishing.

This world measures your success by speed and scale. God measures it by steadiness. And make no mistake, there is a holy glory in finishing what God called you to begin. It doesn't have to look like the world's version of done. It doesn't need a ribbon-cutting or a viral reel. It just needs you and Jesus, hand in hand, at the end of a journey He invited you into.

So whatever you've started (whether it's a business, a project, a calling, or a season), finish it with faithfulness. Because in the Kingdom, that's what leaves a legacy.

Anchor Truth

Philippians 3:13–14 reminds you that growth is not about having arrived, but about releasing what is behind you and intentionally pressing forward

toward the life God is calling you into, with your focus fixed on Christ.

Ecclesiastes 7:8 teaches that the end of a matter is better than its beginning. Patience and perseverance matter more than a fast start.

Hebrews 12:1–2 calls you to run with perseverance the race marked out for you, fixing your eyes on Jesus. He is the pioneer and perfecter of faith.

REFLECTION QUESTIONS

1. Where have I been tempted to quit or give up on something God started through me?

....

....

....

....

2. What does finishing faithfully look like in this current season of my life or business?

....

....

....

....

3. Who could I encourage to keep going this week, just as I've been encouraged?

....

....

....

....

Time Wise Mastery Activity: Faithful Finish Inventory

Take a few moments to look back on this season or this workbook and celebrate the ways you've stayed faithful, even when it was hard. Here are some of my own:

What I Stayed Committed To	Why It Matters
Following through on my client care	Shows consistency and honors the people God brings my way
Creating space for quiet time daily	Keeps me grounded in God, not overwhelmed by the world
Offering my services with excellence	Builds a business that reflects His glory
Trusting God with slow seasons	Develops perseverance and protects my peace

Pro Tip for Busy Women in Business

Identify one thing you started that you're tempted to quit. Ask yourself: "Did God call me to this?" If yes, commit to one more faithful step this week, trusting Him with the outcome.

DECLARATION

I am a finisher. I will not grow weary in doing good. I will complete the work God gave me to do. Even in hard seasons, I will hold on to my hope. Even when the path isn't clear, I will walk by faith. I am not just building a business. I am building for the Kingdom. And by His grace, I will finish faithfully.

PRAYER

Father,

As this week comes to a close, thank You for the confidence You have built within me. Help me carry forward the lessons of trust, obedience, and courage. I commit my future, my work, and my calling fully into Your hands. I walk forward knowing You are with me.

In Jesus' name, Amen.

CLOSING ENCOURAGEMENT

You may not have seen every result yet. You may still be in the middle of the journey. But your heart remains faithful, and Your Father in Heaven sees it. He is not just pleased by what you produce. He is moved by your perseverance. So today, hold your head high and your spirit steady. You are on the path to finishing faithfully.

WALKING FORWARD IN FAITH

This week marked a turning point in your journey—a shift from striving to surrendering, from hesitation to holy action, and from pressure to purposeful obedience.

You have spent the past seven days learning what it truly means to walk in faithful obedience:

- Obedience rooted in trust, not in seeing the full outcome
- Faith strengthened through action, not just meditation
- Vision focused on eternity, not just earthly praise
- Perseverance that keeps walking even when progress feels invisible
- Courage that chooses boldness over comfort
- Surrender that releases outcomes and trusts God's perfect timing
- Endurance that finishes faithfully, not just starts strong

And through each day, one truth has become clearer: Your obedience is never wasted. God sees every faithful step, and He is producing fruit from your faithfulness in ways you cannot yet see.

You are not the same woman you were seven days ago. You've begun walking differently. You're more confident that obedience leads to overflow, more aware that faith grows through movement, more certain that building for eternity matters more than building for approval, more equipped to persevere through slow seasons, more courageous in choosing God's call over cultural comfort, more peaceful in surrendering outcomes to God.

Your calling has started to shift from something you question into something you're learning to walk out with bold, faithful steps.

Obedience is strengthening. Faith is growing. Courage is rising.

This week, you:

- Learned that obedience is your job, and outcomes belong to God
- Strengthened your faith muscle through action, not just belief
- Chose to build with eternity in mind, not external validation
- Kept walking even when you felt stuck or progress felt slow
- Chose courage over comfort and boldness over playing it safe
- Surrendered outcomes and trusted God's perfect process
- Committed to finishing faithfully what God started in you

You didn't just learn more about God's call on your life. You began walking it out.

WHAT YOU'VE LEARNED THIS WEEK

Day 1 — Obedience Over Outcome

Your job is obedience. God handles the outcome. When you take faithful steps, even small ones, God produces fruit in His perfect timing.

Day 2 — Faith Is a Muscle

Faith grows through movement, not meditation. Every small act of obedience strengthens your spiritual muscle and prepares you for what's ahead.

Day 3 — Build with the End in Mind

You're building for eternity, not just earthly applause. What you build in faith lasts forever because it reflects the heart of the King.

Day 4 — When You Feel Stuck, Keep Walking

Movement isn't always fast. Sometimes it's just faithful. Even when progress feels invisible, you are becoming stronger, deeper, and more aligned with God's purpose.

Day 5 — Courage Over Comfort

You weren't called to blend. You were called to burn. Bold obedience is where breakthrough begins, even when your knees shake.

Day 6 — Surrender the Outcome

You can control when and where you plant your seeds, but you cannot control the harvest. When you surrender outcomes to God, you release pressure and receive peace.

Day 7 — Finish Faithfully

The enemy doesn't fear your start. He fears your finish. Finishing faithfully matters more than finishing first or finishing perfectly.

REFLECTIONS FOR THE WEEK

Take a moment today to pause and breathe. Look back over this week and ask yourself:

1. What truth from this week shifted the way I see myself as a woman in business?

....

....

....

2. What area of my business or leadership did I surrender back to God this week?

....

....

....

3. How did I experience God's presence in my work, schedule, or relationships?

....

....

....

4. Where did I feel stretched, and what do I believe God was growing in me through it?

....

....

....

5. What limiting belief, comparison, or fear did I release and lay at the feet of Jesus?

....

....

....

6. What idea, vision, or direction has God started to reveal for my next season?

....

....

....

7. Where am I invited to rest, recharge, and realign before moving forward?

....

....

....

Faithfulness doesn't grow in leaps. It grows in layers. And you have laid a beautiful, solid foundation.

Time Wise Mastery Review: Your Weekly Alignment

Take 20–30 minutes of quiet time to prayerfully answer these check-in questions:

What did I learn this week?

Where did I feel most aligned with God?

What truth am I still wrestling with?

What small win or fruit did I see?

What needs to shift in my mindset, schedule, or systems?

What is God asking me to surrender?

What is God asking me to step into?

Pro Tip for Busy Women in Business

Choose your favorite truth from this week and make it your "obedience anchor" for the next seven days. Put it on your mirror, your phone, or your laptop. Let it steady your spirit every time you're tempted to focus on outcomes instead of obedience.

DECLARATION

I am a woman who obeys before she understands. I choose obedience over outcome, faith over fear, and courage over comfort. My faithfulness leads to overflow, even when I cannot see it yet. I build with eternity in mind, not external validation. I keep walking even when progress feels slow. I surrender outcomes to God and trust His perfect timing. I am not just starting strong. I am finishing faithfully. I am faithfully flourishing by His grace, for His glory.

PRAYER

Father God,

Thank You for leading me through this season of growth and reflection. Thank You for strengthening my faith and reminding me that You are always present in the journey. As I step forward, help me remain anchored in truth and confident in the direction You are leading me.

I place my trust fully in You and release any fear, hesitation, or doubt. I commit my future and my work into Your hands, knowing You are faithful to guide every step.

In Jesus' name, Amen.

CLOSING ENCOURAGEMENT

You're not building alone. You're not hustling for validation. You are co-laboring with Heaven. Keep showing up. Keep obeying from a place of trust. Keep building what only you can build. You are not just someone who started strong. You're someone who is finishing faithfully. And that, my friend, is the legacy of a woman who truly flourishes.

Final Blessing

Dear Beautiful Flourisher,

As you close these pages, I want to remind you that you are not ending a chapter. You are stepping into a new season of purpose.

You are a woman called by God. You are a woman trusted with influence. You are a woman anointed to create, steward, and flourish in ways that echo far beyond what the eye can see.

This journey you are walking, these reflections, these shifts, these seeds sown, are not small things. They are sacred. They are seen by Heaven. And they are already bearing fruit.

You may not see all of the growth yet, but your faithfulness has already been recorded in places that matter most.

You are not just running a business. You are stewarding a calling. You are not hustling for approval. You are flourishing because you are already loved.

I bless you with clarity to recognize God's voice above all the noise.

I bless you with courage to take the next faithful step even when the path ahead is unclear.

I bless you with peace that anchors you when pressure rises.

I bless you with discernment to know what is yours to carry and what to release.

I bless you with holy resilience to stand firm when resistance comes.

I bless you with surrender to trust God's perfect timing, wisdom, and provision.

And above all, I bless you with steadfast faithfulness that honors small beginnings and builds slowly but strong.

May your feet be steady. May your heart be brave. May your spirit be anchored. May your work be excellent. May your faithfulness be unwavering.

Always remember 1 Thessalonians 5:24: "The one who calls you is faithful, and he will do it."

Stay rooted in your identity. Stay surrendered in your plans. Stay wildly expectant for the ways God will continue to multiply what you've entrusted to Him.

You are a light. You are a builder. You are a faithful daughter of the King. And your impact, seen and unseen, is changing the world one obedient step at a time.

Your Father in Heaven is smiling on you. And the best is still unfolding.

With so much love, belief, and celebration for your journey,

Ginger

THE FAITHFULLY FLOURISHING SERIES

This book is part of the *Faithfully Flourishing* Series, a collection created to support women as they grow in faith, confidence, leadership, and purpose across different seasons of life and work.

Each book is designed to stand on its own while also building upon the others, allowing you to enter the journey where you are and move forward as God leads.

Books in the *Faithfully Flourishing* Series

Book 1 – Foundation
Business Growth Series for Women Entrepreneurs

Book 2 – Mindset & Identity
Rooted in Truth, Rising in Purpose

Book 3 – Confidence
Walking Boldly in Your God-Given Assignment

Book 4 – Vision
From Vision to Victory

Book 5 – Balance & Boundaries
Guarding Your Heart, Time, and Energy

Book 6 – Growth
Expanding Your Territory

Book 7 – Resilience
Rising Strong Through Trials

Book 8 – Influence
Leading with Kingdom Impact

Book 9 – Creativity
Unlocking God-Inspired Ideas

Book 10 – Abundance
Living in God's Overflow

Book 11 – Rest
Working from a Place of Peace

Book 12 – Legacy
Building What Lasts Beyond You

To learn more about the series, future releases,
or group opportunities, visit: